Science Explorer

身近な科学の世界

Takayuki Ishii

Masahiko Iwata

Yuko Matsumura

Chinatsu Hirata

Osamu Yamaguchi

Joe Ciunci

photographs by
©iStockphoto.com

音声ファイルのダウンロード／ストリーミング

CD マーク表示がある箇所は、音声を弊社 HP より無料でダウンロード／ストリーミングすることができます。トップページのバナーをクリックし、書籍検索してください。書籍詳細ページに音声ダウンロードアイコンがございますのでそちらから自習用音声としてご活用ください。

https://www.seibido.co.jp

Science Explorer

Copyright © 2019 by Takayuki Ishii, Masahiko Iwata, Yuko Matsumura,
Chinatsu Hirata, Osamu Yamaguchi, Joe Ciunci

All rights reserved for Japan.
No part of this book may be reproduced in any form
without permission from Seibido Co., Ltd.

はじめに

　21世紀になって科学技術は飛躍的な進歩を遂げました。スマートフォンやID技術の素晴らしい発展に加え、「ながらスマホ」という社会現象、さらには、「インスタ映え」などの流行語が発生することなど、20年前には誰も想像すらできなかったと思われます。

　同時に、これから20年後、科学の世界はどう変わるのか、誰も予想できないでしょう。科学技術の発展の理解は、科学のことをもっと知ることから始まり、科学のことを知るには、科学を楽しく学ぶ必要があると思います。

　その科学を楽しく学ぶためには、科学の面白い側面を学ぶことが先決です。そこで、このテキストでは、科学の基礎を学ぶとともに、種々の興味深い側面を学ぶことができるように、編集されています。

　本書は、主として大学の理系学部の英語教育で用いられるテキストとして役に立つだけでなく、雑学的で面白い内容を含んでいるので、文系学部にも適しています。

　本書は、生物・健康・技術・宇宙・数字というテーマについて、4つずつの章を設け、それぞれの章の英文パッセージを中心にさまざまな問題を解く形式の科学分野のリーディング教材です。

　章構成は、段階的にレベルを上げる形になっているので、学生の英語レベルを問わず、楽しく勉強できるようになっています。語彙チェック、Reading、注、内容把握問題、サマリーリスニング、科学雑学コラム、文法チェック、文法解説コラム、ライティング（並べ替え問題）、そしてディスカッションとレベルが上がっていきます。

　本書を通じて、Reading能力の向上のみならず、文法および4技能、とりわけ発信する能力を高めること、そして、同時に科学自体にも興味を高めることにつながれば、著者として，これに勝る喜びはありません。

　本書の制作において、Unit 5 〜 8を岩田が、Unit 12 〜 14を松村が、Unit 3 〜 4およびUnit 10 〜 11を平田が、Unit 9とUnit 19を山口が、Unit 1 〜 2、Unit 15 〜 18とUnit 20、全章の文法コラムとExerciseを石井が、英文パッセージの加筆訂正および全章の校閲をシウンシが、全体の監修を石井が担当しました。

　最後に、本書の制作に当たり、株式会社成美堂の田村栄一氏には企画の段階から有益なご提案と暖かい励ましをいただき、編集の小亀正人氏には具体的なアドバイスと編集において大変熱心にご助力いただき、また、佐藤公雄氏にも原稿を細かにチェックいただきました。企画・編集の際、お世話になった方々に心より感謝申し上げます。

著者代表　石井　隆之

本書の構成と使い方

章構成

各章6ページで、次の①〜⑩の合計 10 の Part に分かれる。

Unit Title 写真 Introduction ① Vocabulary Check	② Reading 本文	③ Notes ④ T/F Questions
1 ページ目	2 ページ目	3 ページ目
⑤ Summary 　Listening ⑥ TIPS	⑦ Grammar Check ⑧ 一口文法	⑨ Writing 　Expressions ⑩ Discussion 　Topics
4 ページ目	5 ページ目	6 ページ目

各 Part の使い方

① Vocabulary Check　8問から成る単語の「英語による定義」を選ぶ問題

② Reading　30 行から 40 行程度の標準的なレベルの英文パッセージ

③ Notes　専門語や分かりにくい単語・熟語・イディオム・特殊な表現の訳やコメント

④ T/F Questions　5問から成る内容把握問題で、正しければ T, 誤りは F を記入

⑤ Summary Listening　10 行〜15 行程度の要約の英文を聞いて穴埋め問題を解く

⑥ TIPS　科学に関する面白い、あるいは注意すべき情報

⑦ Grammar Check　文法力チェック 10 問、選択式・穴埋め・語形変化などの問題

⑧ 一口文法　文法テーマに基づく文法の解説、その章で頻繁に出てきた文法項目を扱う

⑨ Writing Expressions　5問から成る作文問題で、6単語の並べ替えの形式

⑩ Discussion Topics　英語で行うディスカッションのトピック2つを挙げている

目　次

＜生物の話＞

Unit 1　*Is Red a Stimulating Color?* 1
（牛は赤い色に興奮しない?）

Unit 2　*Why Are Giant Pandas Black and White?* 7
（パンダの白黒は竹を食べることと関係がある?）

Unit 3　*Secrets of Primates' Forward-facing Eyes* 13
（霊長類のみ目が前についている本当の理由）

Unit 4　*Why Are Eggs Oval?* 19
（卵がまん丸だったら困る?）

＜健康の話＞

Unit 5　*Can Eyesight Be Improved While We Sleep?* 25
（目の悪さは寝て治せるか?）

Unit 6　*Excessive Intake of Vitamin C Leads to Diarrhea* 31
（ビタミンＣの取り過ぎに注意）

Unit 7　*Mechanism of Sugar Addiction and How to Break It* 37
（人が甘い物を求めるのは自然なこと?）

Unit 8　*Honey Does Not Prevent a Cavity* 43
（蜂蜜は虫歯予防になるか?）

＜技術の話＞

Unit 9　*Future Use of Computers* 49
（コンピューターを再認識する）

Unit 10　*Ice, Pet Cats, Stamps, and Microwave Ovens* 55
（氷を電子レンジに入れたらどうなる?）

Unit 11　*The Unknown Effects of Tatami* 61
（畳のすごさを知る）

Unit 12　*Voice Recognition Sounds Great for Security* 67
（声の生体認証は安全か?）

＜宇宙の話＞

Unit 13 *Will Space Exploration Unlock the Secrets of the Universe?* 73
（太陽系に生命体は存在するのか?）

Unit 14 *Twinkle, Twinkle Little Star — How I Wonder How Bright You Are!* 79
（星の明るさを測る方法は?）

Unit 15 *A Story of Folding Paper* 85
（紙は何回まで折れるか?）

Unit 16 *Is the Tanabata Story Wrong?* 91
（星にとって1年に1回の感覚は?）

＜数字の話＞

Unit 17 *How to Use Numbers in Japanese* 97
（零とゼロの使い方の違い）

Unit 18 *Japan Is Not a Small Country!* 103
（日本は大きな国である!）

Unit 19 *The Sea of Japan* 109
（日本海のことをもっと知ろう）

Unit 20 *The Mystery of 36* 115
（36は不思議な数字!）

Is Red a Stimulating Color?

赤色は情熱の色といわれます。ですから闘争心や革命の色ともされ、共産主義国の旗には赤が使われることが多いものです。闘牛では、牛に赤いマントを見せることにより、牛が興奮しているように見えます。実際はどうなのでしょうか。

Vocabulary Check

次の単語の定義を下の [a] 〜 [h] から選びましょう。

(1) significant (　　)　(2) positive (　　)　(3) perception (　　)
(4) stimulate (　　)　(5) represent (　　)　(6) popularize (　　)
(7) evoke (　　)　(8) spectator (　　)

[a] to be an example, expression or symbol of something
[b] the way you notice things, especially with the senses
[c] a person who is watching an event, especially a sports event
[d] large or important enough to have an effect or to be noticed
[e] to make a lot of people know about something and enjoy it
[f] to make something develop or become more active
[g] feeling confident and hopeful
[h] to bring a feeling, a memory or an image into your mind

From an ethnolinguistic point of view, the color red is one of the four basic colors in Japan, the others being blue, white, and black. Although black and white are generally not considered to be colors, the Japanese language includes them in this category. These four colors share a special Japanese grammar rule. By adding the suffix "i" to the noun form of these colors, the nouns become adjectives. This rule does not apply to other colors.

Red is a significant color in many ways. Red appeals to human emotion and conveys an image of passion and excitement. Red can even help people feel more positive. It also can make time appear to move more quickly.

It is also said that red can even affect humans psychosomatically. Some experiments have shown that when humans are overexposed to the color red, their perception of temperature will rise by one to four degrees. This results from the color stimulating the sympathetic nervous system, leading to active blood circulation and strong pulsation.

The power that red has over the human body isn't lost on advertisers. For example, McDonald's uses red liberally in the interior of its restaurants, the packaging of its goods, and on its website.

The Coca-Cola Company has also capitalized on red. The company chose red for the packaging and advertising of its product because it represents the company's principle of spreading an image of enjoyment and excitement.

Incidentally, the Coca-Cola Company was the first company to dress Santa Claus in red clothes in their advertisements, which helped popularize the image of a red-garbed Santa Claus around the world. It doesn't hurt that his white beard provides a good contrast with the red clothes.

One may draw the conclusion that bulls react strongly to the color red as humans do, as seen in bullfighting in Spain. However, it only seems that the

UNIT 1   *Is Red a Stimulating Color?*

red cape is attracting the bull. In fact, the animal cannot recognize the color, or any color for that matter. Only humans and other primates such as monkeys can see colors. The bull does not react to the bright red cape, but instead to its quick movements in the hands of the matador. If the cloth is not moved, the bull will not charge.   5

It makes sense, then, that any color could be used for the cape in bullfighting. However, only red excites and evokes images of fighting. The entire display is arranged for the sake of the human audience. Therefore, it is not the bull, but the matador and spectators that are excited by the red cape as it is waved wildly in front of the beast.   10

Notes

ethnolinguistic 民族言語学的な / **suffix** 接尾辞 / **noun** 名詞 / **adjective** 形容詞 / **psychosomatically** 心身相関的に（肉体と同時に精神にも影響して）/ **sympathetic nervous system** 交感神経系 / **blood circulation** 血流 / **pulsation** 脈拍 / **be lost on ...** …に影響を与えない；…の心にとまらない / **liberally** ふんだんに / **red-garbed** 赤い服をまとった / **it doesn't hurt that ...** …であっても構わない / **cape** マント（袖なしの短い外套）/ **primate** 霊長類 / **matador** 闘牛士 / **charge** 突進する / **wildly** 激しく

T/F Questions

次の英文が本文の内容と一致する場合は T、一致しない場合は F を記入しましょう。

1. [   ] If the suffix "i" is added to the noun for the color green, it becomes an adjective.

2. [   ] The feeling of time passing quickly is one of the effects that the color red has on our mind.

3. [   ] Generally speaking, most advertisers hate red due to its excessive power.

4. [   ] The Coca-Cola Company was the first firm to come up with a red Santa Claus image.

5. [   ] In bullfighting, it is the movement of the cape that actually excites the bull.

3

Summary Listening

次の英文パッセージは本文を要約したものです。音声を聞いて空所を埋めましょう。

Red, one of the (1.) colors, has a great psychological effect on human beings; therefore, this color is used for many advertisements. In the same way, people tend to think that in bullfighting, red (2.) the bull; as a result, the bull tries to attack the matador.

However, the same is not (3.) of animals. Generally speaking, animals have poor eyesight; the bull is no (4.). In short, bulls cannot see the color red well. The truth is, the bull reacts to the movement of the cape. We can safely conclude that it is not the bright color of the cape but its (5.) movement that agitates the bull.

TIPS

日本文化の重要4色と中国文化の五色

　日本文化において、赤の反対は白ではなく黒です。というのは、赤は「明るい」と関係するのに対し、黒は「暗い」と関係しているからです。赤と黒は明度（明るさ）において対照的なのです。

　一方、白の反対は、黒ではなく青になります。その理由は、白は「著しい」（はっきりしている）から派生した色であるのに対し、青は「淡い」から派生しています。つまり、彩度（鮮やかさ）の視点から対照的な色となるのです。

　ちなみに、赤・黒・白・青に、黄を加えると、中国文化における「五色」となります。中国では、東・南・西・北・中央に、青・赤・白・黒・黄を配置します。すると、不思議なことに、日本文化で対照的となる色の組み合わせ、つまり、青と白、赤と黒が向かい合う関係となります。

UNIT 1   *Is Red a Stimulating Color?*

Grammar Check

次の英文の (　) 内の動詞を正しい形に直しましょう。２語となる場合もあります。

1. I like two colors: One is red, the other (be) blue.   ＿＿＿＿＿

2. Red is considered (be) an auspicious color in Japan.   ＿＿＿＿＿

3. Red also can make time appear (move) more quickly.   ＿＿＿＿＿

4. Some experiments have (show) a very interesting result.   ＿＿＿＿＿

5. The hypothesis of the color (stimulate) the nervous system is often made.   ＿＿＿＿＿

6. The color activates the sympathetic nervous system, (lead) to strong pulsation.   ＿＿＿＿＿

7. McDonald's uses red liberally in the (package) of their goods.   ＿＿＿＿＿

8. The idea of (spread) a good corporate image is very important.   ＿＿＿＿＿

9. It only seems that the red cape is (attract) the bull.   ＿＿＿＿＿

10. The entire display is (arrange) for the sake of the human audience.   ＿＿＿＿＿

一口文法　　**動詞の形**

　英語の動詞の形には、現在形 (do, does)、過去形 (did)、過去分詞形 (done)、現在分詞形 (doing) の４つがある。

　過去分詞形は、have done の形の完了時制や be done の形の受動態で用いられ、現在分詞形は be doing の形の進行時制で用いられる。

　英語には、主語の人称や数などによって語形の制限を受けず、名詞や形容詞、副詞の役割をする準動詞というものがあり、「不定詞」(to do)、「動名詞」(doing)、「分詞」(現在分詞形の doing と過去分詞形の done をまとめたもの) の３種類に分類できる。

準動詞	名詞的用法	形容詞的用法	副詞的用法
不定詞	～すること	～するための	～するために
動名詞	～すること	×	×
分詞	×	語は前から句は後から名詞を修飾	分詞構文

5

Writing Expressions

次の英文の (　　) 内の単語を並べ替えて、英文を完成させましょう。

1. 心理学的な視点から、興味深いことを述べたいと思います。
   Let me tell you something interesting (a / from / of / point / psychological / view).

   _____

2. 色は人間の心に大きな影響を与えると言われています。
   Colors are said (a / great / have / influence / on / to) human minds.

   _____

3. 唾液の分泌は、私たちの体が毒を取り除こうとすることによって起こります。
   The secretion of saliva (body / from / our / results / to / trying) get rid of the poison.

   _____

4. それは全く間違いであるという結論を導く人がいるかもしれません。
   Some (conclusion / draw / may / people / that / the) it is completely wrong.

   _____

5. 本当のことを言うと、私が好きな色は、青ではなく、赤です。
   To tell you the truth, it (blue / but / is / not / red / that) I like.

   _____

Discussion Topics

次の質問に答えることをきっかけとして、英語で話し合いましょう。

1. What color do you like best? And why?

   _____

2. Is there anything you are excited about? Tell me more about it.

   _____

Why Are Giant Pandas Black and White?

パンダが白黒なのは、自らを目立たせて威嚇するためだとか、逆に周りの景色になじんで見つかりにくくするためだとか、黒い色が熱を吸収し体温調節に役立つからだとか、実に色々な説があります。しかし最近は、新しい説が出てきました。いったいどんな説でしょうか。

Vocabulary Check

次の単語の定義を下の [a] 〜 [h] から選びましょう。

(1) fur (　　)　　(2) wonder (　　)　　(3) ancestor (　　)
(4) evolve (　　)　　(5) consume (　　)　　(6) hibernate (　　)
(7) conspicuous (　　)　　(8) relevant (　　)

[a] to eat or drink something
[b] very easy to notice or likely to attract attention
[c] the thick mass of hair that grows on the body of an animal
[d] to gradually develop from simple to more complicated forms
[e] closely related to the subject in question or to the situation at issue
[f] an animal that lived in the past from which a modern animal has developed
[g] to have some kind of interest in knowing about something due to it being not known well
[h] to spend the whole winter in a physical state of deep sleep by storing a lot of energy

7

The baby giant panda Shang Shang was quite popular among visitors to Ueno Zoo in 2018. Japanese find giant pandas to be much cuter than other types of bears. This is no doubt due to their black and white fur and rotund bodies. The black legs on a white chubby-looking body and black patches around the eyes and over the ears make giant pandas irresistible to many.

One must wonder why giant pandas are black and white while other bears are not. There may be a variety of theories; however, recent studies suggest that they are black and white because of their bamboo diets.

Generally, 99% of a giant panda's daily diet consists of bamboo, or more precisely, the leaves, stems and shoots of various bamboo species. However, the animal's ancestors may have eaten meat; after all, they are bears, which are carnivores taxonomically. We should note that around 90% of bears at present mainly eat plants and nuts due to the way they have evolved.

A glacial period existed around 20 million years ago. During that time, the ancestors of the giant panda lost out in the fierce struggle to secure meat for survival. As a result, they were forced into wooded areas to find food to sustain them. They started to consume bamboo, which conveniently grew all year round.

With a diet consisting almost solely of bamboo, giant pandas became unable to hibernate. In order to hibernate during the four-month winter, they would have to eat more than 20,000 kilocalories of food every day – an impossible feat for them because of the low caloric intake a diet of bamboo provides.

Instead of hibernating, pandas were forced to scour the forests for bamboo throughout the year. Originally, they were black; therefore, in winter they must have really stood out in clear contrast with the white snow. Gradually, their fur adapted to their environment and became whiter to blend with the snow.

UNIT 2   *Why Are Giant Pandas Black and White?*

However, if pandas had become totally white, they would have looked conspicuous again while foraging in the dark forests in summer. Eventually, their fur became black and white so that they could partially blend in no matter the season.

Interestingly, other animals are not able to easily notice a giant panda, 5 even if it is big, because their eyesight is not keen enough to pick out the mottled black-and-white-furred bear. To another animal, the giant panda would not stand out at all from the scenery.

With the giant panda, we can clearly see evolution at work. The color of their fur is due to their unique eating habits. The concept of "you are what you 10 eat" is certainly relevant here.

Notes

rotund 丸々とした / **chubby** 太ってかわいい / **irresistible** 愛らしい，魅力的な / **carnivore** 肉食動物 / **taxonomically** 分類学上 / **glacial period** 氷河期 / **feat** 芸当，偉業 / **low caloric intake** カロリー摂取が少ないこと / **scour** 急いで探し回る / **forage** (食べ物を) 探し回る / **mottled** まだらの，斑点がある / **you are what you eat** 何でも食べ物で決まるものだ [←直訳：あなたは食べる物からできている]

❄ · · · ❄ · · · ❄ · · · ❄ · · · ❄ · · · ❄ · · · ❄ · · · ❄ · · · ❄ · · · ❄ · · · ❄ · · · ❄

◉ T/F Questions

次の英文が本文の内容と一致する場合は T、一致しない場合は F を記入しましょう。

1. [   ] There are only a few theories as to why giant pandas are black and white.

2. [   ] When giant pandas first went into the forest, they didn't eat bamboo.

3. [   ] Giant pandas' inability to hibernate is due to their eating low-calorie bamboo.

4. [   ] Giant pandas' fur was white originally but gradually became blacker.

5. [   ] The color of giant pandas' fur is a good example of "you are what you eat."

次の英文パッセージは本文を要約したものです。音声を聞いて空所を埋めましょう。

　Giant pandas have risen in popularity. This may be due to their cutely (1.　　　　　　　) black and white fur. According to a recent theory, the reason they are black and white is related to their eating habits.

　In the remote past, their ancestors lost out in the struggle for meat and had to (2.　　　　　　　) to the woods, where bamboo grew. However, since the calorie intake from bamboo is not (3.　　　　　　　) to sustain hibernation, they had to forage over a wide area for food every day.

　Their originally black fur gradually turned whiter so that they might be less conspicuous in the winter snow, while in the dark forest, some of their coat remained black to better (4.　　　　　　　) with the vegetation. In short, the combination of black and white was a result of (5.　　　　　　　).

TIPS

動物の進化 --- 犬と猫の分岐点

　約6500万年前から4000万年前ごろまで、犬と猫の共通の祖先であるミアキスという動物が森にすんでいました。3000万年前ぐらいになると、気候変動で森が減少し、草原が増えてきました。この草原地帯へ移りすんだのが、犬の祖先となりました。草原では敵に容易に見つかるので、群れを成して行動するようになり、群れの中では、序列意識も生まれ現在の犬の特徴を持つようになります。

　一方、森に残ったのが猫の祖先で、森では隠れるところが多いので、集団で身を守る必要はなく個別に活動します。そして、木登りなどの技術が上達します。現在の猫の特徴が現れてくるのです。

　草原に出るか、森に残るかの違いで、犬と猫の差が生まれたわけです。

UNIT 2   *Why Are Giant Pandas Black and White?*

◉ Grammar Check

次の英文の (　) に入る適切な前置詞を、下の枠内から選びましょう。選択肢のなかには、繰り返して使うものもあります。また、前置詞が不要なものもあります。

1. The reason why giant pandas are cute is due (　　　) their black and white fur.

2. There may be a variety (　　　) theories regarding why they are black and white.

3. Instead (　　　) hibernation, pandas were forced to search the forests for food.

4. Their fur adapted (　　　) their environment, becoming whiter to blend with the snow.

5. When we do research on the giant panda, we can clearly see evolution (　　　) work.

6. The red leaves on maple trees in the temple were in clear contrast (　　　) the blue sky.

7. The sea otters you see in the zoo are really irresistible (　　　) many visitors there.

8. The currently established planning committee consists (　　　) nine members.

9. I will continue to do what I decided to do at that time (　　　) no matter the situation.

10. Shintaro studied English very hard; (　　　) a result, he became a very good English speaker.

at	as	in	of	to	with

一口文法　**前置詞とその前後**

　前置詞は、名詞句の前に置かれる品詞なので「前置詞」と呼ばれる。前置詞は、名詞・形容詞・副詞・動詞の後にも付いて、その前置詞の直後の名詞句とつなぐ役割をしている。副詞の後に付く例として、instead of... out of...、differently from... などがある。

　一般に、前置詞は関わる名詞・形容詞・副詞・動詞によって異なる。例えば、influence には on、afraid には of、away には from、focus には on が付く。名詞の場合は、前の前置詞との関わりも重要である。on the occasion、in the situation のように好まれる前置詞がある。前置詞の位置と他品詞（内容語）の関係を示しておく。

前置詞の位置	名詞	形容詞	副詞	動詞
前に付く	○	×	×	×
後に付く	○	○	○	○

11

Writing Expressions

次の英文の（　　）内の単語を並べ替えて、英文を完成させましょう。

1. コアラはなぜユーカリの葉だけを食べるのか、と人は不思議に思うに違いありません。
   One (eat / koalas / must / only / why / wonder) eucalyptus leaves.

   _____

2. 私がそう発言する理由はいろいろありますが、1つ理由を述べます。
   There (a / are / of / reasons / variety / why) I say so, but let me give you one.

   _____

3. 食べる物のほとんどが竹なので、パンダは冬眠が不可能だったのです。
   With (a / almost / consisting / diet / of / solely) bamboo, pandas couldn't hibernate.

   _____

4. もしコアラがユーカリを常食としなかったら、何が起こったでしょうか。
   If (always / eaten / eucalyptus / had / koalas / not), what would have happened?

   _____

5. 彼らは、ユーカリを解毒するのに十分な睡眠を取る必要がなくなったでしょう。
   They would not have (a / enough / long / needed / sleep / to) detoxify eucalyptus poison.

   _____

Discussion Topics

次の質問に答えることをきっかけとして、英語で話し合いましょう。

1. What animal do you like best? Give three reasons.

   _____

2. What eating habits do you recommend?

   _____

Secrets of Primates' Forward-facing Eyes

ヒトは霊長類に属します。「霊長」とは何かを知っていますか。霊長類とは、霊長目（サル目とも言う）の哺乳類の総称です。霊長とは、「霊妙な力を備えていて、他の中で最も優れているもの」という意味があります。つまり、ヒトやサルなどは他の哺乳類とは異なり、人知では計り知ることのできない最も優れている哺乳類だといえるのです。

Vocabulary Check

次の単語の定義を下の [a] 〜 [h] から選びましょう。

(1) contrast (　　)　　(2) stare (　　)　　(3) game (　　)
(4) rely (　　)　　(5) motion (　　)　　(6) interpret (　　)
(7) advantage (　　)　　(8) feature (　　)

[a] to look steadily with the eyes wide open
[b] something that helps you to be more successful than others
[c] the movement of something
[d] wild animals, birds or fish that are hunted for food
[e] a typical quality of something
[f] to put together different objects to show their differences
[g] to explain the meaning of something
[h] to depend on someone or something to do what you need

A common characteristic amongst all primates is their eye structure. The foreheads of other animals are angular with eyes on the sides, not in front, so that each eye can see in different directions. In contrast, the forehead of primates is flat, and they have forward-facing eyes that stare in the same direction. A primate's forward-looking eyes use a technique called triangular surveying to measure the approximate distance of an object by differentiating between two points, which makes it easy to see depth.

The eyes of animals such as a leopard or a lion are on the sides of their head to allow a wide range of view to search for game. On the other hand, as with grazing animals such as deer, a wide-angle view allows them to easily detect a potential attack by a predator.

Other animals can quickly perceive and track the subtle or suspicious movements of other animals, either game or beasts of prey, by using their eyes; their nose is used only to search for game for consumption by relying on sensitive olfactory perception.

Incidentally, the fingerprint, of which no two patterns are alike, is a sole characteristic of primates. This fingerprint is called a dermal ridge because the print is made by an impression of the ridges on the skin of the finger. Primates are the only animals that have this dermal ridge, which enables them to effectively grip objects.

Ridges create frictional force between an object and the fingers, but this force alone is not strong enough to prevent objects from slipping out of one's fingertips. Nerve endings and sweat glands are concentrated in the fingertips. The moist ridges add extra viscosity to a grip and the nerves help the primate identify what it is holding.

Not to lose sight of what we were initially discussing, but Homo sapiens

UNIT 3   *Secrets of Primates' Forward-facing Eyes*

have more eye white than other primates, and accordingly the pupils are relatively small, resulting in the iris being able to move along a wider plane. This contributes to efficiency, since it allows someone to look at something without having to turn the head or body as much.

It is theorized that the white of the eye grew larger as people tended 5 to communicate while looking at each other. The motion of the eye is more apparent with large whites, so subtle movements can be interpreted and add to the ability to effectively communicate. In fact, all primates have this ability. Orangutans, for example, take full advantage of this feature to communicate effectively. As you can see, there's a lot more to eyes than one may think. 10

Notes

triangular surveying 三角測量 / **grazing animal** 草食動物 / **predator** 捕食動物 / **track** 跡を追う / **beast of prey** 肉食獣 / **olfactory perception** 嗅覚 / **fingerprint** 指紋 / **dermal ridge** 皮膚隆線 / **nerve endings** 神経末端・神経終末 / **sweat gland** 汗腺 / **viscosity** 粘度, 粘着性 / **pupil** 瞳 / **iris** 虹彩 /**orangutan** オランウータン

❈ · · · ❈ · · · ❈ · · · ❈ · · · ❈ · · · ❈ · · · ❈ · · · ❈ · · · ❈ · · · ❈ · · · ❈

◉ T/ F Questions

次の英文が本文の内容と一致する場合は T、一致しない場合は F を記入しましょう。

1. [   ] A common characteristic among all primates is their sensitive noses.
2. [   ] A primate's forehead is angular with eyes on the sides.
3. [   ] A leopard has forward-facing eyes to search for game.
4. [   ] Fingerprints are possessed only by humans.
5. [   ] Orangutans can communicate effectively by using their eyes.

次の英文パッセージは本文を要約したものです。音声を聞いて空所を埋めましょう。

The fact that a primate's forehead is not angular but flat (1.   ) it to perceive the distance of an object accurately. In contrast, animals like leopards have their eyes on the sides of their heads to be able search for (2.   ) over a wide field of vision.

One more characteristic unique to a primate is that it has fingerprints unlike other members of the animal (3.   ). The ridges on its skin which form its fingerprint (4.   ) it to effectively grip an object.

Homo sapiens are highly evolved among primates, with a greater amount of white in their eyes. This is because eyes play an important role in communication as subtle movements can (5.   ) various messages.

TIPS

人類の進化 --- ホモサピエンスとネアンデルタール人

ネアンデルタール人は、ホモサピエンスよりも6ミリほど大きな目をしていたようです。これは脳が視覚に特化しており、判断能力は劣っていた可能性を示唆します。約2万5000年前、氷河期が到来した時、ネアンデルタール人は、従来と同じように大きな動物を狙っていたため、その大型動物の死滅とともに滅んでしまったとみられます。

一方、ホモサピエンスは、食べ物を求めて、それまでは口にしたことがなかった貝類などを食べるようになりました。これが、氷河期を生き延びることにつながったと考えられます。つまり、食べることができるかもしれないという「好奇心」があったことが、絶滅を回避したと考えられるのです。

UNIT 3   *Secrets of Primates' Forward-facing Eyes*

🌐 Grammar Check

次の英文の (　　) 内の語 (句) うち正しい方を選びましょう。

1. In (contrast / the contrast), the forehead of a primate is flat.

2. A primate can measure the approximate distance of (object / an object).

3. Triangular surveying makes it easy to see (depth / a depth).

4. (Wide / A wide) range of view is possible if you use this special camera.

5. Many animals use their nose to search for (game / a game).

6. The fingerprint is a dermal ridge on (a skin / the skin) of the finger.

7. An eagle is classified as a bird of (prey / the prey).

8. Be careful not to lose (sight / the sight) of your life goals.

9. (An / The) ability to effectively communicate is important in our life.

10. Humans take (full / the full) advantage of the motion of their eyes.

一口文法　　冠詞の種類と冠詞の要不要

　冠詞には不定冠詞 (a と an) と定冠詞 (the) の 2 種類がある。an は母音の発音で始まる単語の前に付く。

　不定冠詞は、不特定の 1 つや 1 人を表し、定冠詞は特定の物や人 (単数・複数は問わない) を表す。

　名詞は、可算名詞 (数えることができるもの) と不可算名詞 (数えることができないもの) に大別できる。不可算名詞の代表は物質名詞で、固有名詞は通常不可算。抽象名詞は 1 つのまとまりを感じさせるものについては可算名詞となる。

　可算名詞・不可算名詞と冠詞の関係は以下の通り。(N は名詞 / -s は複数を表す)

	不定	定
単数	a + N	the + N
複数	N-s	the + N-s

＜可算名詞＞

	不定	定
単数	N	the + N

＜不可算名詞＞

Writing Expressions

次の英文の (   ) 内の単語を並べ替えて、英文を完成させましょう。

1. 両目のそれぞれが異なる方向を見ることができるように進化した動物は多い。
   Many animals developed in a way (can / each / eye / in / see / that)
   different directions.

   _____

2. その動物は潜在的な攻撃を簡単に予測することが可能な眼を持っている。
   The animal has eyes (allow / detect / easily / it / to / which) a potential
   attack.

   _____

3. 指紋は霊長類のみが持つ特徴である。
   The fingerprint (a / characteristic / is / of / primates / sole).

   _____

4. 人間は、動物が突然襲ってくるのを防ぐことができるほど強くはない。
   Humans are not (animals / enough / from / prevent / strong / to)
   attacking suddenly.

   _____

5. 人間は意思伝達の努力のおかげで、瞳を動かすことが可能になった。
   Humans' effort to communicate (able / being / in / iris / resulted / the)
   to move.

   _____

Discussion Topics

次の質問に答えることをきっかけとして、英語で話し合いましょう。

1. Do you think humans are superior to other animals? Why or why not?

   _____

2. Is there anything you bear in mind to communicate well with your friends
   or other people?

   _____

Why Are Eggs Oval?

卵は、日本には、2000年以上も前に中国から朝鮮半島経由で伝えられました。昔から卵は貴重な食べ物です。冷蔵庫に卵がストックされるようになるのは1950年代後半で、比較的最近のことだそうです。本章では、卵がなぜ楕円形なのかについて学びます。

Vocabulary Check

次の単語の定義を下の [a] 〜 [h] から選びましょう。

(1) environment (　　) (2) predator (　　) (3) prevent (　　)
(4) contain (　　) (5) quite (　　) (6) efficient (　　)
(7) typically (　　) (8) existence (　　)

[a] to a large extent
[b] to stop from doing something
[c] the surroundings in which a person or animal lives.
[d] in a way that shows the expected features of something or someone
[e] to have something inside
[f] the state of being present in a particular place or situation
[g] able to do things well and properly
[h] an animal which lives by hunting, killing, and eating other animals

The environment in which eggs incubate contributes greatly to their oval shape. In the cutthroat world of nature, eggs and the chicks depending on them wouldn't be able to survive if not protected. Luckily, birds with the ability to fly can make a nest on the boughs of high trees or on the ledges of cliffs to protect their young from predators.

There are three reasons why eggs are oval: in other words, three conditions which prevent them from being perfectly spherical.

First, it is necessary for eggs to not be able to easily fall from a nest. Birds nurture their young in high up places where they can be safe from hungry predators, but there is a risk of eggs rolling out of a nest. If eggs were spherical like balls, they would easily roll out of a nest after being nudged; however, as an egg is oval-shaped, it can wobble back to its original position in the nest.

Secondly, an oval shape is necessary to allow young birds to easily hatch from the eggs. This is because the rounder part of the egg, called the air chamber, has a space that contains air. This space grows larger and the surrounding shell becomes softer than the pointed ends as the young bird grows. This thin part of the egg shell is easy to break, so a newborn chick can hatch from there quite easily.

Finally, an oval shape makes efficient use of space in a nest. Birds lay their eggs at high altitudes where space is naturally limited. It is there that they warm the eggs to full maturity. Typically, there can be several eggs in any one nest. If eggs are spherical, there would be unused space between each egg. However, since one side of each egg is pointed, space between eggs is minimized as they lie on their sides with the pointed ends facing towards the center.

In conclusion, as discussed above, we have learned that there are some practical reasons for eggs being oval. The mere existence of the air chamber

UNIT 4   *Why Are Eggs Oval?*

mentioned earlier is also proof that the egg itself breathes. The egg takes in air through the thinner shell of the air chamber area. Therefore, if an egg is stored in a refrigerator with the rounded part upward and its pointed part downward, the egg can be kept fresh for a longer period. Isn't this all "egg-citing"?

> **Notes**
>
> **incubate** ふ化する / **cutthroat** 厳しい / **bough** 大枝 / **ledge** （絶壁から突き出た）岩棚 / **spherical** 球形の / **nurture** 育てる / **nudge** 押しのける / **wobble** ふらふらする / **hatch** 鳥が卵からひなをかえす / **air chamber** 気室 / **altitude** 標高 / **maturity** 成熟期 / **minimize** 最小限にする / **egg-citing** たま [ご] げた [exciting をもじったジョーク]

❋ ・ ・ ・ ❋ ・ ・ ・ ❋ ・ ・ ・ ❋ ・ ・ ・ ❋ ・ ・ ・ ❋ ・ ・ ・ ❋ ・ ・ ・ ❋ ・ ・ ・ ❋ ・ ・ ・ ❋ ・ ・ ・ ❋ ・ ・ ・ ❋

⬤ T/F Questions

次の英文が本文の内容と一致する場合は T、一致しない場合は F を記入しましょう。

1. [   ] The environment in which eggs incubate is responsible for their oval shape.
2. [   ] Birds can make a nest on the boughs of a high tree.
3. [   ] If eggs were not oval-shaped, they would easily roll out of nests.
4. [   ] The existence of an air chamber does not prove that eggs breathe.
5. [   ] If we store an egg in a refrigerator with the pointed part upward and its rounded part downward, the egg will remain fresh.

次の英文パッセージは本文を要約したものです。音声を聞いて空所を埋めましょう。

We can safely say that the environment has played a (1.   ) in an egg's oval shape. This will be clear once we know the three reasons why eggs are oval.

First, eggs are oval so that they will not (2.   ) from a nest. The oval shape enables the egg to (3.   ) back to its original position.

Secondly, the oval shape makes the egg's rounder base grow thin so that a newborn chick can easily break through to (4.   ).

Lastly, the fact that eggs are oval makes it possible for them to be close to each other due to a more (5.   ) use of space, since all the pointed ends usually face towards the center of a nest.

TIPS

六角形の不思議

　自然界には六角形がたくさん見つかります。例えば、雪の結晶、蜂の巣、トンボの複眼、ミクロの世界ではベンゼン環などがあります。六角形は特別な形で、安定しています。同じ形を平面に敷き詰める場合に可能な形は、三角形・四角形・六角形の3種類しかないのですが、六角形が最も安定して動くことはありません。このことが自然界に六角形があふれる理由だと考えられます。

　ビニール袋をシャボン玉でいっぱいにして平面に押しつけると、シャボン玉は六角形になります。六角形は、物理的にも優れた形なので、人工物にも応用されています。鉛筆の断面、ボルトの頭、サッカーゴールのネットなどに利用されています。

UNIT 4　　*Why Are Eggs Oval?*

⬤ Grammar Check

次の英文の (　　) 内の語 (句) のうち正しい方を選びましょう。

1. Eggs' oval shape is closely related to the environment in (that / which) eggs incubate.

2. There are three reasons (where / why) eggs are oval.

3. There are three conditions (which / whose) prevent eggs from being spherical.

4. Birds nurture their young in places (where / which) they can be safe.

5. The rounder part of the egg has a space (that / who) contains air.

6. Birds lay their eggs at high altitudes (on which / where) space is limited.

7. It is at high altitudes (that / which) birds warm their eggs to full maturity.

8. (As / Which) discussed above, we can draw a certain conclusion successfully.

9. We have learned (that / which) there are some practical reasons for eggs being oval.

10. The mere existence of the air chamber is proof (that / which) the egg breathes.

一口文法　　関係詞その1

　関係詞は、接続詞と他の品詞 (名詞、形容詞、または副詞) の2つの役割をする。
　関係詞の種類と形は、先行詞と，その関係詞 (を含む句) が後続する文において
どんな役割をするかによって決まる。

先行詞と関係詞が導く文における役割から見た関係詞　 (P＝前置詞)

先行詞	主格	所有格	目的格	副詞
人	who	whose	who(m)	P + whom
物 (時・場所・理由を含む)	which	whose of which	which	P + which
人・物	that	—	that	×
時	—	—	—	when
場所	—	—	—	where
理由	—	—	—	why, that
句、節、文	which ＊	—	which ＊	×

　＊ 非制限用法で用いる。

23

Writing Expressions

次の英文の（　　）内の単語を並べ替えて、英文を完成させましょう。

1. 卵がふ化する環境が、その楕円形の大きな原因となっている。
   The environment where eggs (contributes / hatch / greatly / oval / their / to) shape.

   _____

2. 飛ぶ能力を持つ鳥は、高いところに巣を作ることができる。
   (ability / birds / fly / the / to / with) can make a nest at high altitudes.

   _____

3. 卵が巣から簡単に落ちることができないということが必要である。
   It is necessary for eggs to (able / be / easily / fall / not / to) from a nest.

   _____

4. 卵内の幼い鳥が成長するにつれ、卵の丸い部分が柔らかくなる。
   The rounder part of the egg becomes (as / bird / in / the / softer / young) the egg grows.

   _____

5. 昆虫がそれなりの形をしていることには、実用的な理由がいくつかある。
   There are several practical reasons (being / for / in / insects / shaped / their) own way.

   _____

Discussion Topics

次の質問に答えることをきっかけとして、英語で話し合いましょう。

1. Which shape do you like better, a circle or triangle? Or, is there any shape you particularly like? And why?

   _____

2. What do you think you should be most careful about in your life?

   _____

Can Eyesight Be Improved While We Sleep?

視力矯正法は眼鏡かコンタクトレンズが一般的でした。近年はレーザー手術も普及してきています。しかし、寝ている間に視力が回復する方法があるそうです。どのような方法なのでしょうか。興味が湧きませんか。

Vocabulary Check

次の単語の定義を下の [a] 〜 [h] から選びましょう。

(1) corrective (　) (2) alter (　) (3) blur (　)
(4) athlete (　) (5) obtrusive (　) (6) hazardous (　)
(7) tissue (　) (8) elasticity (　)

[a] undesirably prominent
[b] participants in a sport
[c] to obscure or to dim
[d] the ability of an object to resume its normal shape after being stretched or compressed
[e] to make something different in size, style, course, etc.
[f] designed to make something right that was wrong before
[g] any of the distinct types of material of which animals or plants are made
[h] involving a risk or danger, especially to someone's safety or health

Wouldn't it be great if everyone could have 20/20 vision? Because of advancements in medical technology, there is actually a way to improve your vision as you sleep. Typically, one must resort to using corrective eyewear or contact lenses to compensate for poor vision. Laser eye surgery is also an option. None of these choices improve eyesight while you are sleeping, however. Then what does? The answer is orthokeratology.

Orthokeratology is an overnight vision correction method. It requires a person to wear specially designed contact lenses that alter the shape of the cornea. The lenses correct nearsightedness, or myopia, and can even help cure blurred vision, or astigmatism. Orthokeratology lenses are worn only while sleeping and allow the person to go contactless during the day.

How is this possible? By shaping the cornea, orthokeratology lenses improve vision. In other words, the lenses change the refraction rate of the cornea. The cornea is altered enough that the wearer will see the benefits the next day.

These lenses are especially attractive to people who do not want to wear glasses or contacts during the day. Athletes find them advantageous as they can compete without having to wear obtrusive eyewear. Orthokeratology is effective for not only athletes but also children. The number of children who suffer from myopia has increased significantly in recent years. Glasses can be awkward and even hazardous for active children. Contact lenses have to be prepared and applied carefully, something most children will struggle with. Laser eye surgery is not without its dangers. Orthokeratology is currently considered the ideal option for myopic children.

Another advantage is that changes due to orthokeratology are reversible. Laser eye surgery, on the other hand, is irreversible because the process

UNIT 5 *Can Eyesight Be Improved While We Sleep?*

removes corneal tissue. The elasticity of the cornea means that everything will return to normal after a few days of not wearing the lenses. This can also be disadvantageous, however, as the lenses must be applied every night to maintain the benefits.

Overall, orthokeratology is a relatively safe way to fix myopia. It can be used as needed and stopped anytime. This treatment, however, has a short history of usage and more data is necessary before we can make any concrete conclusions about its benefits and drawbacks.

Notes

20/20 vision 正常な視力 / **orthokeratology** オルソケラトロジー（視力矯正方法の１つ）/ **cornea** 角膜 / **nearsightedness** 近視 / **myopia** 近視（↔ hyperopia 遠視）/ **blurred vision** かすみ目 / **astigmatism** 乱視 / **refraction** ［物理学］屈折 / **drawback** 欠点

T/F Questions

次の英文が本文の内容と一致する場合は T、一致しない場合は F を記入しましょう。

1. [　　] Orthokeratology is the only method to correct myopia.
2. [　　] Orthokeratology corrects nearsightedness temporarily.
3. [　　] People must wear orthokeratology lenses while they are awake.
4. [　　] Wearers of orthokeratology lenses enjoy their advantages immediately after starting to use them.
5. [　　] Even if people stop wearing orthokeratology lenses, their eyesight remains good enough.

次の英文パッセージは本文を要約したものです。音声を聞いて空所を埋めましょう。

　Advancements in medical technology enable people to fix certain conditions once considered to be incurable. The (1.　　　　　) of orthokeratology, for example, has allowed people to retrieve 20/20 vision overnight without surgery. (2.　　　　　) to ordinary contact lenses, orthokeratological lenses must be worn during the night; in other words, while people are sleeping.

　Orthokeratological lenses are specially designed contact lenses that change the shape of the cornea. The lenses change the refraction (3.　　　) of the cornea and allow good vision as long as the shape is maintained. Poor vision will return after the (4.　　　　　) method is stopped; it is reversible. This overnight vision correction method is a (5.　　　　　) safe way to correct eyesight immediately.

TIPS

近視は進化？

　現代人の仕事の多くはコンピューターに向かうデスクワークです。昔に比べて近くを見ることが多くなりました。近くを見るための進化が近視なのかもしれません。狩りを営む地域の人の視力は驚異的です。遠くまで見えなければ生命が危険にさらされる状況下では、目が進化して遠くが見えるようになるはずです。

　マサイ族の戦士は数キロ先のブッシュに潜むライオンをも判別できるそうです。一説にその視力は、6.0 を超えるともいわれています。しかし、マサイ族が住む地域においても、近年はスマホなどの電子機器も普及してきているそうで、何年か先には視力が低下する可能性があります。

UNIT 5   *Can Eyesight Be Improved While We Sleep?*

Grammar Check

次の英文の（　）に入る適切な接続詞または接続副詞を下の枠内から選びましょう。選択肢のなかには、繰り返して使うものもあります。

1. It would be great (　　　　　) everyone in our office could have 20/20 vision.

2. People with poor eyesight usually wear glasses (　　　　　) contact lenses.

3. None of the above-mentioned choices improve eyesight (　　　　　) you are sleeping

4. The lenses can even help cure blurred vision, (　　　　　) astigmatism.

5. Generally speaking, people grow wiser (　　　　　) they get older.

6. The method is effective for not only athletes (　　　　　) also children.

7. Glasses can be awkward (　　　　　) even hazardous for active children.

8. Another advantage is (　　　　　) changes due to orthokeratology are reversable.

9. The boss was unable to attend the meeting (　　　　　) he was hospitalized.

10. I was very late for the dinner party. There was, (　　　　　), plenty left for me.

and	as	because	but	however	if	or	that	while

🗨 **一口文法**　　**接続詞と接続副詞**

　2つの文を接続する品詞として、接続詞と接続副詞がある。
　接続詞には、等位接続詞と従位接続詞があり、後者には2種類の形式がある。接続副詞には、3種類の形式がある。
　代表的な順接と逆接を例に取り、具体例を挙げる。　　　　　　　　[A, B は文]

先行詞	順接　（A だから B である）	逆接　（A だけれど B である）
等位接続詞	and, so ⇒ A and B.	but, yet ⇒ A but B.
従位接続詞	as, since, because ⇒ Because A, B. [=B because A.]	though, although ⇒ Though A, B. [=B though A.]
接続副詞	therefore ⇒ A. Therefore, B. 　[=A; therefore, B.]	however ⇒ A. However, B. 　[=A; however, B.]

　※接続副詞のもう1つの形式は、上記の B=SV... として、A. S, therefore, V... のように文中に割り込む形式。

29

Writing Expressions

次の英文の（　　）内の単語を並べ替えて、英文を完成させましょう。

1. 色々な本を読めば、知識不足を埋め合わすことができるだろう。
   You can (by / compensate / for / lack / knowledge / of) reading a variety of books.

   _____

2. 彼女は教授から与えられた難しい課題に挑んでいる。
   She is (assignment / challenging / given / struggling / the / with) by the professor.

   _____

3. その社長はほぼ非論理的とみられる行為に訴えた。
   The president (act / as / regarded / resorted / the / to) almost illogical.

   _____

4. ラーメンは今や日本の食文化の一部であると考えられている。
   Ramen is (be / considered / currently / of / part / to) Japanese food culture.

   _____

5. 腰痛を患う若者の数が増えてきている。
   The number of young people (backache / been / from / has / suffer / who) increasing.

   _____

Discussion Topics

次の質問に答えることをきっかけとして、英語で話し合いましょう。

1. How many hours do you usually sleep? What do you think is your ideal sleeping time?

   _____

2. Is there any method you take to get rid of the stress? Tell me more about it.

   _____

Excessive Intake of Vitamin C Leads to Diarrhea

ビタミンCを摂取することは、健康に良いとされています。ビタミンCを含んだ飲料やグミ、飴、サプリメントなど、多種多様な商品が販売されています。しかし、過剰摂取すると体に異変が起こるそうです。いったいどのような変化が起きるのでしょうか。

Vocabulary Check

次の単語の定義を下の [a] ～ [h] から選びましょう。

(1) proverb (　) (2) nutrition (　) (3) diet (　)
(4) overuse (　) (5) messy (　) (6) issue (　)
(7) susceptible (　) (8) soak (　)

[a] to lie in and become saturated or permeated with water or some other liquid
[b] to use too much or too often
[c] the process by which organisms take in and utilize food material
[d] a short popular saying
[e] food and drink considered in terms of its qualities, composition, and its effects on health
[f] admitting or capable of some specified treatment
[g] characterized by a dirty, untidy, or disordered condition
[h] a point in question or a matter that is in dispute, as between contending parties

Reading

   The old proverb says we are what we eat. That is, the food we eat directly affects our health. Most people have a basic knowledge of nutrition; however, it is not necessarily reflected in what they eat. There are many readily available sources of nutrition such as vitamin and mineral supplements, energy drinks, and breakfast cereals. Many people rely on these to enhance their diets. However, overuse based on a lack of knowledge about vitamins can lead to some very messy problems.

   Vitamin C is one of the most essential nutrients and one that we need every day. It helps to repair and regenerate tissue, prevent scurvy, combat cancer, fight the common cold, and so forth. Vitamin C deficiency, on the other hand, results in fatigue, bleeding gums, and joint and muscle pain. In severe cases, a shortage causes scurvy. Vitamin C, therefore, is necessary to maintain our health.

   Our body neither produces nor stores vitamin C, so we must eat foods and supplements with a sufficient amount each day. However, a diet too high in vitamin C can cause a problem. Vitamin C is a water-soluble vitamin; therefore, any amount not used will be excreted from the body. While going a little overboard with vitamin C won't cause any issues, having an excessive amount can lead to diarrhea.

   The amount of vitamin C needed to cause diarrhea does not come from a normal diet. Vitamin C is susceptible to heat, oxygen, and water so the amount of the vitamin in foods is dramatically reduced by cooking. Soaking spinach in water for five minutes decreases its vitamin C content by 20%. Boiling the spinach for three minutes will reduce the vitamin C by half. Even though cooking diminishes the amount of vitamin C in foods, the recommended daily dose of 100mg is still easily achievable without going too far over the limit. It is said that taking in more than 2,000mg of vitamin C per day may cause diarrhea. A person would be full before eating enough foods with a sufficiently high vitamin C content to cause the runs. Therefore, supplements seem to be the main reason for vitamin C overdoses. It is relatively simple to exceed safe amounts of vitamin C if one takes too many vitamin pills or tablets. Excessive dependence on supplements may actually inflict serious damage on our bodies. Nutrition specialists, therefore, recommend that we get our nutrition from food rather than supplements or energy snacks.

Sound knowledge of nutrition helps us to choose the proper foods and amounts we should eat. A balanced intake of vitamins is essential for our health. Eating normally should provide us with all that we need for a healthy life.

Notes

diarrhea 下痢 / **messy problem** 厄介な問題 / **regenerate** 再生する / **scurvy** 壊血病 / **fatigue** 疲労 / **gum** 歯茎 / **joint** 関節 / **water-soluble** 水溶性 / **excrete** 排泄（はいせつ）する / **go overboard** ［口語］夢中になる / **spinach** ホウレンソウ / **the runs** 下痢 / **overdose** 過剰投与 / **sound** 十分な；確実な根拠のある

T / F Questions

次の英文が本文の内容と一致する場合は T、一致しない場合は F を記入しましょう。

1. [   ] The excessive intake of vitamin C always leads to diarrhea.
2. [   ] Lack of vitamin C will cause a variety of diseases.
3. [   ] Vitamin C is diminished by cooking.
4. [   ] Nutrition specialists advise people to get nutrition mainly from supplements.
5. [   ] With a proper knowledge of nutrition, one can choose healthy foods.

次の英文パッセージは本文を要約したものです。音声を聞いて空所を埋めましょう。

　The food we eat directly (1.　　　　　　) our health. Although quite a few people have a basic knowledge of nutrition, it is not necessarily reflected in what they eat. Many people rely on readily available sources of nutrition such as (2.　　　　) supplements to enhance their diets. However, poor knowledge about vitamins can lead to serious problems.

　Vitamin C is one of the most (3.　　　　　) nutrients. Unfortunately, our body neither produces nor stores vitamin C, so we must eat foods and supplements with a sufficient amount each day. However, an (4.　　　　　　　) amount leads to diarrhea. Vitamin C is susceptible to heat, oxygen, and water, so the amount of the vitamin in foods is dramatically reduced by cooking. Only (5.　　　　　) lead us to take it in excessive amounts. A balanced diet with appropriate knowledge of nutrition helps us to stay healthy.

TIPS

サプリメントは Cash Cow?

　ドラッグストアに行くと、どれを選べばよいか分からないくらいにサプリメントが並んでいます。異業種の大手企業もこの業界に参入しています。富士フイルムは、かつては写真フィルムを主力商品として製造していた会社ですが、今はサプリメントが主力事業になっています。

　今ではすっかりサプリメントや化粧品で有名になった DHC ですが、前身は大学翻訳センターで、大学の研究室を顧客として翻訳事業を営んでいました。

　時代の変化とともに企業も生き物のように変化していることがうかがえます。

UNIT 6 *Excessive Intake of Vitamin C Leads to Diarrhea*

Grammar Check

次の英文の (　) 内の単語のうち正しい方を選びましょう。

1. The food we eat (direct / directly) affects our health.

2. This book may be useful; (however / therefore), it is too expensive.

3. Our good knowledge of a language is (no / not) necessarily reflected in our ability to speak it.

4. Overuse of vitamins may lead to some (much / very) messy problems.

5. Vitamin C, (because / therefore), is necessary to maintain our health.

6. (But / However), a diet too high in Vitamin C can cause a problem.

7. John is a man of talent; (otherwise / therefore), I will assign this task to him.

8. Mary went a bit (much / too) far in her criticism about Jack's behavior.

9. Bob tends to take (far / too) many vitamin pills or tablets.

10. Eating (abnormally / normally) should provide us with all we need for a healthy life.

一口文法　副詞その1　形からの分類

副詞は名詞以外を修飾する品詞である。
典型的には、動詞、形容詞、副詞といった内容語を修飾する。
形から大きく4分類できる。

(a) LY で終わる副詞、主として形容詞から派生する。例：quiet → quietly

(b) 動詞と組み合わせて用いる副詞、前置詞と同形もある。例：in、out、away など。

(c) 特殊な形を持つ副詞、主に前から形容詞や動詞を修飾する。
形容詞を修飾する例：very、too、far など。
動詞を修飾する例：always、usually など（頻度副詞など）。

(d) 時を表す副詞、名詞と同形であることが多い。例：yesterday、every day など。

⬤ Writing Expressions

次の英文の（　　）内の単語を並べ替えて、英文を完成させましょう。

1. ビタミンＣは私たちが毎日必要な最も基本的な栄養素の１つである。
   Vitamin C (essential / is / most / one / of / the) nutrients we need every day.

   _____

2. 私たちの体はビタミンＣを作り出すことも蓄積することもできないといわれている。
   It is said that (body / neither / nor / our / produces / stores) Vitamin C.

   _____

3. 活性酸素の増加がいくつかの病気の主な原因と思われる。
   An increase in active oxygen (be / for / main / reason / seems / the / to) some diseases.

   _____

4. サプリメントよりも食物から栄養を取ることが勧められている。
   It (get / is / our / recommended / that / we) nutrition from food rather than supplements.

   _____

5. 世界で起きていることに関するしっかりとした知識があれば、安全な海外旅行を計画するのに役立つことは間違いない。
   Sound knowledge of what is going on in the world (a / helps / plan / surely / to / us) safe trip abroad.

   _____

⬤ Discussion Topics

次の質問に答えることをきっかけとして、英語で話し合いましょう。

1. Do you usually take supplements? Why or why not?

   _____

2. Is there any particular method you take to keep fit? Tell me more about it.

   _____

Mechanism of Sugar Addiction and How to Break It

甘いものに目がないという人も多いのではないでしょうか。大手コーヒーチェーンが提供する呪文のような長い名前のコーヒーも多量の砂糖を含んでいます。カフェインにも依存性がありますが、砂糖の依存性も無視できないほどの影響があるそうです。

Vocabulary Check

次の単語の定義を下の [a] 〜 [h] から選びましょう。

(1) satisfy (　)　(2) perk (　)　(3) thrive (　)
(4) scavenge (　)　(5) carbohydrate (　)　(6) evidence (　)
(7) crave (　)　(8) substance (　)

[a] to gain in vigor or cheerfulness
[b] grounds for a belief; or proof
[c] to ask for something earnestly
[d] to eat anything that can be found
[e] a fundamental or characteristic part or quality
[f] to grow strongly and vigorously
[g] one of the important nutrients that provides your body with heat and energy
[h] to fulfill a need, desire, or expectation

Reading

Eating for pleasure is nothing new. Most of us prefer sweet things over bitter or sour foods. Evolutionary psychology teaches us that human beings instinctively have a natural sweet tooth. While eating sweets every now and then may satisfy us and even perk us up a bit, it is possible to become dangerously addicted to sugar.

Our desire for sweet foods has been with us since the dawn of humanity. The ancestors of humans were able to survive and thrive by scavenging fruits and berries. A sweet taste meant the food was ripe and safe to eat, while bitter and sour tastes meant it could be poisonous or unripe. Carbohydrates are a source of energy and essential for healthy body and brain function. Humans that ate sweet, healthy foods rich in carbs lived longer lives and had more offspring. These offspring were born with a desire to eat sweet foods.

Sugar is an efficient provider of carbohydrates, for which we all have natural cravings. A small spoonful of sugar usually provides enough carbs to quell cravings. However, there is neurochemical scientific evidence that shows it is possible to become addicted to sugar. A person may crave sugar the same way a person craves illegal drugs. This is due to sugar releasing opioids and dopamine in the human body, both contributing to addiction.

There are many types of substances that can cause addiction for different reasons. Some, such as alcohol and the nicotine in tobacco, are well-known addictive substances that are widely abused. Some lead to a strong dependence; others, a lesser dependence. The degree of dependence, however, does not necessarily correlate with the legality of the substance. Nicotine, for instance, is legal, but is more addictive than marijuana. And though nicotine and alcohol are legal, they lead to such high dependency that withdrawal from them takes a lot of effort.

UNIT 7　*Mechanism of Sugar Addiction and How to Break It*

Research shows that the brain begins to respond to sugary food before it enters the mouth. Seeing the food stimulates the brain's reward center. As soon as the food touches the tongue, taste buds send signals to the brain, which in turn responds by emitting the neurochemical dopamine, resulting in an intense feeling of pleasure. Sweets saturate the brain with too much dopamine, and 5 so the brain eventually adapts by becoming desensitized. This desensitization diminishes the number of cellular receptors that recognize and respond to the neurochemical. Therefore, the brain consequently demands more sugar to release dopamine.

Breaking any addiction is not easy. Addiction must be understood 10 and treated as a disease and not a matter of willpower. A strong will alone is not enough to prevent or cure addiction. Instead, treatment by a medical professional that has knowledge and experience treating addiction is necessary.

Notes

evolutionary psychology 進化心理学 / **have a sweet tooth** 甘党である / **dawn** 夜明け / **unripe** 熟していない / **carb**=carbohydrate / **quell** 抑える / **neurochemical** 神経化学の / **opioid** オピオイド（麻薬性鎮痛作用を有する物質の総称）/ **dopamine** ドーパミン / **nicotine** ニコチン / **marijuana** マリフアナ / **withdrawal** 使用中止，離脱 / **taste buds** 味蕾（みらい：舌の上皮にある味覚器官）/ **saturate** 満たす / **desensitize** 鈍感にする / **desensitization** 鈍感化 / **cellular receptor** 細胞受容体

●T/F Questions

次の英文が本文の内容と一致する場合は T、一致しない場合は F を記入しましょう。

1. [　] Human beings have loved sweets since the dawn of the species.

2. [　] Our ancestors could discern edible foods from inedible foods by their taste.

3. [　] The intake of carbohydrates was closely related to reproduction in ancient times.

4. [　] A spoonful of sugar may lead to addiction, which results in using illegal drugs.

5. [　] As addiction is a matter of willpower, it shouldn't be treated as a kind of disease.

39

 **Summary Listening**

次の英文パッセージは本文を要約したものです。音声を聞いて空所を埋めましょう。

　　Evolutionary psychology has (1.　　　　　) why human beings prefer sweets. Our ancestors distinguished edible foods from inedible foods by taste. Sweet foods such as fruit are healthy. Also, a (2.　　　　　) amount of our carbohydrates come from sugar; therefore, we have natural cravings for sugar. However, sugar can (3.　　　　　) addiction.

　　Studies show that the brain responds to (4.　　　　　) foods before they enter the mouth. Taste buds also send signals to the brain soon after the substances touch the tongue. Dopamine is released during this entire process. The brain gradually becomes (5.　　　　　) to the stimulation and as a result requires more sugar. It is impossible to break addiction by willpower alone. Addiction should be treated by medical professionals.

TIPS

多岐にわたる依存症

　依存症には主に2種類あります。物質への依存とプロセスへの依存です。物質への依存には薬物、アルコール、たばこなどがあり、プロセスへの依存にはギャンブル、買い物などがあります。

　依存症は本人の意志の問題と思われがちですが、病気として扱い、治療しなければなりません。脳が強い刺激を覚えてしまうと、それ以上の刺激を求めてしまうため、治療が非常に難しいのが厄介なところです。

UNIT 7 *Mechanism of Sugar Addiction and How to Break It*

Grammar Check

次の英文の（　　）内の語（句）のうち正しい方を選びましょう。

1. Eating for the sake of pleasure is nothing (new / newly).

2. Most of us prefer sweets over (bitter / better) or sour fruit.

3. It is possible to become dangerously (addict / addicted) to sugar.

4. Sugar is an (efficient / efficiently) provider of carbohydrates.

5. He doesn't have (enough / more enough) sense to realize his serious mistakes.

6. It is (possibility / possible) for her to get there in time.

7. The brain begins to respond to (sugar / sugary) food before it enters the mouth.

8. Sweets saturate the brain with too (many / much) dopamine.

9. This tall tree may not be (ease / easy) for any monkey to climb.

10. An operation is (necessary / necessity) if the patient is to recover.

一口文法 　**形容詞**

形容詞は名詞を修飾する役割をする品詞である。
形容詞と名詞の位置関係として、次の2つがある。
　前置修飾：形容詞→名詞　　　例：scientific evidence、a beautiful flower
　後置修飾：名詞←形容詞（句）　例：something new、a man afraid of dogs

用法としては、以下の2種類がある。
　限定用法：名詞の意味を限定する　例：a strong dependence
　叙述用法：主語または目的語を説明する　例：Alcohol is legal. / It made her happy.

それぞれの用法しかない場合があるので注意すべきである。
　限定用法のみの形容詞：mere（単なる）、only（唯一の）
　叙述用法のみの形容詞：asleep（眠って）、well（元気な）、glad（うれしい）

※限定用法は永続的な性質を表し、叙述用法は一時的な状況を意味する。

41

Writing Expressions

次の英文の (   ) 内の単語を並べ替えて、英文を完成させましょう。

1. 人は違法薬物を求めるのと同じように、砂糖が欲しくなるようである。
   A person seems to crave sugar (a / craves / person / same / the / way)
   illegal drugs.

   _____

2. しわの量は、必ずしも実年齢との相関性が高いとは言えない。
   The amount of wrinkles (correlate / does / necessarily / not / well / with)
   the actual age of a person.

   _____

3. ニコチンやアルコールはやめるのに大変な努力が必要となるほどの高い依存性に
   つながる。
   Nicotine and alcohol lead to such high (dependency / from / requires /
   that / them / withdrawal) a great deal of effort.

   _____

4. 甘い食べ物が舌に触れるとすぐに、私たちは強い喜びの感情を抱く。
   As (as / food / soon / sugary / the / touches) tongue, we get an intense
   feeling of pleasure.

   _____

5. 依存症は、病気として認識され，治療されなければならない。精神力の問題では
   ない。
   Addiction must be understood and treated as a disease and (a / matter /
   not / of / power / will).

   _____

Discussion Topics

次の質問に答えることをきっかけとして、英語で話し合いましょう。

1. Do you have a sweet tooth? What sweets do you like best and why?

   _____

2. Is there anything you think you should not do but cannot give up?

   _____

42

Honey Does Not Prevent a Cavity

蜂蜜は古来から薬として各家庭で常備薬のように使用されてきました。養蜂自体もかなり長い歴史があるそうです。そんな蜂蜜ですが、蜂蜜を食べれば虫歯にならないといううわさがあるようです。甘いものを食べると虫歯になるイメージがありますが、真偽はどうなのでしょうか。

Vocabulary Check

次の単語の定義を下の [a] 〜 [h] から選びましょう。

(1) ancestor (　) (2) evaporation (　) (3) prescription (　)
(4) application (　) (5) anecdotal (　) (6) acid (　)
(7) oral (　) (8) aspect (　)

[a] change from a liquid to a vapor
[b] based on personal observation, rather than scientific evaluation
[c] related to the mouth
[d] a chemical substance that has a pH of less than seven
[e] a particular status or phase in which something appears
[f] an act of putting something to use
[g] one from whom a person is descended
[h] a written direction for a therapeutic or corrective agent

 **Reading**

Apiculture, or beekeeping, has a longer history than one might think. Our ancestors began to domesticate wild bees in the Middle East about 9,000 years ago. Various methods of apiculture have continued throughout the world since then. Bees produce honey from floral nectar with the help of enzymes and water evaporation. The harvested honey has long been recognized as a valuable resource that is naturally preservable.

Historically, honey has been considered medicinal. According to the ancient Egyptian Ebers papyrus, which dealt with medical matters, honey was included in prescriptions for internal and external applications. It has also been widely used in traditional Ayurveda medicine in India as well. According to Ayurveda, honey fights infections, heals wounds and burns, relieves diarrhea, suppresses coughing, reduces stress, eliminates sleeping disorders, and cures bad breath. It seems honey is a cure-all; however, some of the effects might be anecdotal with no scientific evidence.

It is rumored that honey prevents tooth decay. To understand how this is possible, we must first discuss the types of honey. There are three kinds available: pure honey, sweetened honey, and distilled honey. Pure honey is natural, taken directly from bee hives. Sweetened honey is diluted with sweeteners such as starch. Distilled honey is boiled in a distillery and extracted. Of these, only pure honey is considered to contain sufficient antibacterial substances. This means that only pure honey may work to prevent tooth decay.

Honey does not completely prevent tooth decay; it simply works to weaken the bacteria present. No antibacterial substances are able to eliminate all bacteria in an oral cavity. The surviving bacteria may still cause tooth decay. The rumor that honey prevents tooth decay is therefore true only to a certain extent.

UNIT 8   *Honey Does Not Prevent a Cavity*

Acid is another cause of decay. Tooth decay can occur in an acidified oral cavity. Honey, unfortunately, does not neutralize or alkalize the oral cavity. However, cheese does reduce acid in the mouth and is said to prevent tooth decay. In this case, honey does not play a significant role.

One might be tempted to think of honey as a panacea; however, it does have   5
some negative aspects. Honey should not be given to infants, more specifically children under 12 months old. It may also contain botulinus, a microbe which exists in nature and causes food poisoning. Also, the availability of pure honey has been decreasing, causing prices to rise. It is fine to include honey in one's diet, but it is wise to lower one's expectations regarding its beneficial aspects.   10

Notes

cavity 虫歯 / **apiculture** 養蜂 / **domesticate** 飼いならす / **floral nectar** 花蜜 / **enzyme** 酵素 / **Ayurveda** アーユルベーダ / **sleeping disorder** 睡眠障害 / **cure-all** 万能薬 / **distilled** 蒸留された / **dilute** 薄める / **antibacterial** 抗菌性の / **acidify** 酸性化する；すっぱくする / **neutralize** 中和する / **alkalize** アルカリ化する / **panacea** 万能薬 / **infant** 幼児 / **botulinus** ボツリヌス菌 / **microbe** 微生物

❋ · · · ❋ · · · ❋ · · · ❋ · · · ❋ · · · ❋ · · · ❋ · · · ❋ · · · ❋ · · · ❋ · · · ❋ · · · ❋

◉ T/F Questions

次の英文が本文の内容と一致する場合は T、一致しない場合は F を記入しましょう。

1. [   ] The domestication of wild bees in the Middle East dates from 9,000 years ago or so.

2. [   ] Either enzymes or water evaporation are essential for honey production.

3. [   ] Honey has been used as a flawless panacea all over the world.

4. [   ] Honey kills all bacteria; however, it cannot prevent tooth decay.

5. [   ] Tooth decay in infants cannot be prevented by the application of honey.

45

次の英文パッセージは本文を要約したものです。音声を聞いて空所を埋めましょう。

Apiculture has a long history. Bees produce honey from floral nectar using enzymes and water evaporation. Honey has been used as a kind of panacea both in Egypt and India. Honey is said to prevent (1.　　　　　) decay. There are three kinds of honey, but only pure honey might be beneficial in this way.

Although honey does not completely (2.　　　　　) tooth decay, it (3.　　　　　) the bacteria present. So, the rumor that honey prevents tooth decay is only partially true. Tooth decay can occur in an acidified (4.　　　　) cavity. Honey does not neutralize or alkalize the cavity. Honey is safe to eat; however, it shouldn't be given to (5.　　　　　) because it might contain a poisonous microbe called botulinus. Although the price of honey is increasing, it is expected to remain a part of our diet despite not being a cure-all.

TIPS

ニホンミツバチはスズメバチを撃退する

蜜蜂は大きく分けるとニホンミツバチとセイヨウミツバチがあります。ニホンミツバチは比較的小さく、セイヨウミツバチに比べると、蜜を集める量も多くはありません。

しかし、セイヨウミツバチはスズメバチに襲われた場合、打つ手はなく全滅しますが、ニホンミツバチは蜂球を作り、体を動かし熱を出し、スズメバチを熱で殺して巣を守ります。これは、スズメバチが耐えられる熱が、ニホンミツバチが耐えられる熱よりも少しだけ低いため可能なのです。

Grammar Check

次の英文の(　)内の単語を正しい形にしましょう。

1. (Vary) methods of apiculture have continued since wild bees began to be domesticated.　　　　　　　　　　　　_____

2. (History), honey has been believed to have many medicinal effects.　　　　　　　　　　　　　　　　　　_____

UNIT 8 *Honey Does Not Prevent a Cavity*

3. Honey has been (wide) used in traditional Ayurveda medicine in India.

   _____

4. There are three kinds of honey (avail): pure honey, sweetened honey, and distilled honey.

   _____

5. Pure honey is a kind of honey that is (direct) taken from bee hives.

   _____

6. My favorite food is a boiled egg that has an inside that hasn't become (complete) solid.

   _____

7. Honey (simple) works to weaken the bacteria present.

   _____

8. (Unfortunate), what you are looking for is out of stock.

   _____

9. Honey should not be given to infants, more (specific) children under 12 months old.

   _____

10. It is wise to lower our expectations concerning (benefit) aspects of honey.

   _____

一口文法　副詞その２　文副詞

　同じ副詞でも、動詞句を修飾する様態副詞と文全体を修飾する文副詞の両方の機能を持つものがあることに注意すべきである。
　　She expressed her thanks naturally.
　　（彼女は素直に謝意を表明した）[様態副詞]
　　Naturally, she expressed her thanks.
　　（彼女の謝意の表明は当然のことだった）[文副詞]

文副詞には、4 種類ある。
　(a) 主語とその行為を評価する副詞：
　　　Carelessly he drank the water. （不注意にも、彼はその水を飲んでしまった）
　(b) 命題についての確信度を示す副詞：
　　　She probably won't say such a thing. （彼女は多分そんなことを言わない）
　(c) 状況を評価する副詞：
　　　He, unfortunately, was injured in the accident.
　　　（残念なことに彼は事故でけがをした）
　(d) 命題に対する態度を示す副詞：
　　　Honestly, he is no gentleman. （正直言って、彼はちっとも紳士ではない）

　※ 様態副詞は、否定文や疑問文の前に来ないが、文副詞の (a)(b)(c)(d) は否定文の前に
　　来ることが可能で、(d) は疑問文の前にも来る可能性がある。ただし曖昧性がある。
　　Honestly, what did you say at the meeting?
　　（意味 1）　正直に聞くよ。その会議で何を言ったの。[正直なのは話者]
　　（意味 2）　正直に言ってね。その会議で何を言ったの。[正直になるべきは聞き手]

47

Writing Expressions

次の英文の（　　）内の単語を並べ替えて、英文を完成させましょう。

1. 養蜂は予想外に長い歴史を持っている。
   Apiculture has a (history / longer / might / one / than / think).

   _____

2. ミツバチは酵素の力の助けを借りて、花蜜から蜂蜜を作る。
   Bees produce honey from (floral / help / nectar / of / the / with)
   enzymes.

   _____

3. 新規採用の部長はかなりのやり手といううわさだ。
   It is (employed / manager / newly / rumored / that / the) is quite a go-
   getter.

   _____

4. 蜂蜜が虫歯を予防するといううわさは、ある程度までは当たっている。
   The rumor that honey prevents tooth decay is (a / certain / extent / only /
   to / true).

   _____

5. 納豆は万能の食品と考える人がいるが、やはりマイナスの側面がいくつかある。
   Some people think of natto as a panacea, but (aspects / does / have / it /
   negative / some).

   _____

Discussion Topics

次の質問に答えることをきっかけとして、英語で話し合いましょう。

1. Is there any particular insect you like and why?

   _____

2. What do you think is the healthiest food in the world and why?

   _____

Future Use of Computers

世界には実にさまざまな文化がありますが、文明は1つであるといわれます。その1つの文明とはコンピューター文明です。スマホは持ち歩きできるコンピューターとはいえ、今では電話機能以外に、インターネット、Eメール、写真、動画撮影、音楽鑑賞、ゲーム、財布機能、メモ機能など実にさまざまなことが可能です。この章では、コンピューターについて再考しましょう。

Vocabulary Check

次の単語の定義を下の [a] ～ [h] から選びましょう。

(1) military (　)　(2) hardware (　)　(3) generate (　)
(4) vehicle (　)　(5) radiation (　)　(6) interior (　)
(7) patient (　)　(8) physical (　)

[a] energy that is given off in the form of waves or very tiny particles
[b] having to do with matter and energy
[c] having to do with the armed forces, soldiers, or war
[d] a means of carrying or transporting people or goods
[e] the machinery or equipment needed to do something
[f] to bring about or produce
[g] the inner part of something
[h] a person who is under the care or treatment of a doctor

Today's computers function faster than ever and are loaded with features, but nobody can accurately imagine what computers of the future will be like. Originally, the computer was developed to perform complex calculations and aid in the development of the hydrogen bomb, as well as calculating artillery trajectories for the military. Once mass-produced, the computer became an invaluable tool for those in business and engineering. Nowadays, developers and engineers continue to find new ways to use it, such as in moviemaking, robotics, military hardware, and the medical field.

Computers are able to add special effects to movies that would have once been thought of as impossible. It didn't take long after the advent of the modern PC for 3D computer-generated imagery to be used in films. These 3D enhanced images are lifelike and add to the appeal of the films while allowing story writers to stretch the boundaries in terms of setting and what characters are capable of.

Another area computers excel in is robotics. Many scientists are working on intelligent robots whose abilities could one day surpass those of humans. To do this, engineers have focused on artificial intelligence, which the robots will use to assist humans with their jobs. They could help at financial institutions, perform customer service roles, and work in the public sector, such as at police departments.

Researchers are also very keen on using computers for military matters. They are developing new unmanned remote-controlled drones as well as intelligent robots to fight alongside human soldiers. Developing robotic vehicles, which could get into hazardous places without having to worry about people being harmed, is also a major research focus.

Finally, X-rays and CT scans use radiation to produce images of the interior of a human body to search for abnormalities. X-rays allow physicians to view things from one perspective, while CT scans use computer technology to take several X-ray images that are two-dimensional cross-sections and turn them into a multidimensional picture that can be used to make a diagnosis. These single X-rays are combined using computer programs that precisely reconstruct the internal structure of the patient.

Magnetic resonance imaging, more commonly known as MRI, is the process of using powerful magnetic fields to map the patient's internal structure. Bioelectrical activity in the body is detected by a machine that feeds it to a computer that interprets the structure of the area being scanned and presents a three-dimensional presentation of electrical activity in the region. This allows doctors to search for physical and operational defects in patients without invasive surgery.

There's no telling what the future will bring, but it's a sure bet that computers will continue to be a big part of it.

Notes

artillery 大砲 / **trajectory** 軌道 / **robotics** ロボット工学 / **medical field** 医療分野 / **special effects** 特殊効果 / **advent** 出現 / **imagery** 画像 / **lifelike** 実物そっくりな / **artificial intelligence** 人工知能 / **financial institutions** 金融機関 / **remote-controlled** 遠隔操作の / **abnormality** 異常な状態・部分 / **diagnosis** 診断，分析 / **bioelectrical activity** 生体電気活動 / **feed A to B** A（データなど）と B（コンピューターなど）に送り込む / **three-dimensional 3** 次元の / **invasive surgery** 侵襲的手術（生体を傷つけるような手術）

T/F Questions

次の英文が本文の内容と一致する場合は T、一致しない場合は F を記入しましょう。

1. [   ] The computer recently became an essential tool for Japan's military industry.

2. [   ] Many years had passed until computer-based 3D imagery was used in movies.

3. [   ] Very few scientists are developing robots that could one day outsmart humans.

4. [   ] CT scans use radiation to make images of the inside of a patient, but not X-rays.

5. [   ] MRI enables doctors to look for abnormalities in patients without invasive surgery.

 **Summary Listening**

次の英文パッセージは本文を要約したものです。音声を聞いて空所を埋めましょう。

We live in an age of computers. Computers were originally used for military purposes and to quickly (1.   ) through data in the business world. Today, engineers are (2.   ) new uses for computers, such as in moviemaking, robotics, military hardware and in the medical field.

Computers enable filmmakers to make the (3.   ) real with computer enhanced effects. Robotics is another popular field that (4.   ) on computers. Also, computers are being used on the front lines with soldiers. Computers remain important for medical use, such as with X-rays and CT scans. MRI, or Magnetic Resonance Imaging, uses powerful (5.   ) fields to map the patient's internal structure – something possible only with the use of computers.

TIPS

未来のコンピューター

コンピューターが wearable（身に着けられる）になってきています。腕時計型のコンピューターはすでに開発されており、眼鏡やコンタクトレンズもコンピューターになり、目の前の空間に画面が現れる形式も出てくるでしょう。瞬時に多言語間を翻訳する機器も出現するでしょう。

2070年以降になると、心で思うだけでコンピューターやロボットが操作可能になると考えられています。脳をスキャンしたり、記憶をクラウドにアップロードしたり、そのクラウドから他人の記憶を自分の脳にダウンロードしたりすることが可能な時代が来るかもしれません。他人の脳の記憶をすべて、自分の脳にダウンロードしたら、自分はいったい何者になるのでしょうか。

UNIT 9   *Future Use of Computers*

Grammar Check

次の英文の ( ) 内の語 (句) うち正しい方を選びましょう。

1. Nobody (can / cannot) accurately imagine what will happen in the next 20 years.
2. I am quite interested in what the future's computers (will / shall) be like.
3. Computers (are able / enable) to cope with enormously complicated calculations.
4. Computers can add special effects to movies that (will / would) have once been thought of as impossible.
5. Many scientists are working on intelligent robots whose abilities (could / need) one day surpass those of humans.
6. CT scans use computer technology to turn several X-ray images into a multidimensional picture that (can / do) be used to make a diagnosis.
7. I haven't heard from her for more than three years. Something (cannot have / must have) happened.
8. My boyfriend (should / ought) have known better than to argue with my father, who is quite a debater.
9. If they can come to an understanding, they (need not / do not need) bring the matter before the court.
10. My close friend (has / will have) been to the United Kingdom ten times if he goes there next week.

一口文法 助動詞

助動詞とは動詞の原形の前に付いて、動詞が表す意味を補助する役割をする品詞である。

基本的には、(a) 聞き手に対する働き掛けと (b) 話者の心的態度の2つの意味を併せ持つのが、典型的な特徴である。どちらも「気持ちを表すこと」に関わる。

	can	may	should	must	will
(a)	[可能性] できる	[許可] してよい	[提案] すべき	[命令] しないといけない	[意志未来] するつもり
(b)	あり得る possibly occasionally	かもしれない perhaps sometimes	はずだ probably often	違いない certainly usually	する [単純未来]、なる [推量] だろう

※ (b) の2行目は確信度を示す副詞、3行目は頻度の副詞との対応を示す。[will 以外]

Writing Expressions

次の英文の（　　）内の単語を並べ替えて、英文を完成させましょう。

1. 実物そっくりの３Ｄイメージは映画の魅力を増す。
   The lifelike 3D (add / appeal / images / of / the / to) the films.

   _____

2. 研究者は軍事関連でコンピューターを使用することに非常に関心がある。
   Researches are (computers / for / keen / on / using / very) military matters.

   _____

3. 物事をいくつかの視点から見るということは極めて重要なことである。
   It is of utmost (from / importance / several / things / to / view) perspectives.

   _____

4. ソリュブルコーヒーは、もっと一般的にはインスタントコーヒーとして知られている。
   Soluble coffee (as / commonly / instant / known / is / more) coffee.

   _____

5. 未来がどうなるかは分からないが、ロボットはさらに進化するだろう。
   There is no (bring / future / telling / the / what / will), but robots will develop more.

   _____

Discussion Topics

次の質問に答えることをきっかけとして、英語で話し合いましょう。

1. What is the most convenient point about the use of computers and why?

   _____

2. Tell me what you think Japanese society will be like in 20 years.

   _____

Ice, Pet Cats, Stamps, and Microwave Ovens

「電子レンジでチンする」…この言葉は、かつての電子レンジは調理終了の音が「チーン」だったことに由来します。現在の電子レンジは音がチーンとは限りませんが、電子レンジは本当に便利ですね。電子レンジに氷を入れたらどうなるのでしょうか。本章では、そんな単純な疑問への回答を含め、人気の電子レンジの使い方、裏技などを学びます。

Vocabulary Check

次の単語の定義を下の [a] ～ [h] から選びましょう。

(1) misguide (　　)　　(2) interact (　　)　　(3) object (　　)
(4) stupid (　　)　　(5) explode (　　)　　(6) electron (　　)
(7) aside (　　)　　(8) revert (　　)

[a] to talk to each other or have an effect on each other
[b] out of the way
[c] something that can be seen or touched
[d] to burst with a loud noise
[e] to lead someone to something wrong
[f] to go back
[g] showing lack of good sense or judgement
[h] a very small piece of matter with a negative electrical charge that goes around the central part of an atom

According to an urban legend, when a cute pet cat came home all drenched on a rainy day, its misguided owner put the poor thing into a microwave to dry it off. Whether this story is true or not, people have tried using microwave ovens for a variety of things, with all kinds of different results.

In a microwave oven, electric waves called microwaves interact with water molecules causing them to vibrate rapidly. The temperature rises as the molecules continue to vibrate. The heat of the water molecules is transmitted to other molecules, and the total temperature of the object increases. It is through this process that an object is heated.

Therefore, if someone was stupid enough to put a wet pet in a microwave oven, it would burn to death quite horribly. In fact, there are many things which should not be put in a microwave oven, for example, food with shells intact or food wrapped in an airtight film or covering. This means that eggs or sausages should not be overly heated because they may explode due to vapors being unable to escape when the temperature rises.

Metallic objects such as aluminum foil catch fire almost instantly in microwave ovens. This is because metal contains electrons that can move freely, so thermal conduction occurs dangerously fast. It is therefore never a good idea to heat up metal in a microwave.

Microwave ovens do have some uses aside from cooking. When old lumpy sugar is put in a microwave in an oven-proof dish without any wrapping and heated for one minute, it will revert back to its granular form as if good as new. A microwave oven is also useful for taking off postage stamps that have been stuck on by mistake. After moistening the stamp and warming it in the oven for 20 seconds, it will peel off easily. Soaking a sponge with water and heating it in a microwave is a good way to sterilize it. Who knew microwaves

UNIT 10   *Ice, Pet Cats, Stamps, and Microwave Ovens*

could be so useful?

Now here's something to consider – what would happen if ice is heated in a microwave oven? Will the ice melt immediately, or will the vapor-filled air suddenly explode due to the intense heat given off by the oven?

Neither answer is correct. The microwaves in the oven do not react with the water molecules in ice the same way they do with liquid water. Surprisingly, the ice will not melt! This is because water is heated approximately 8,000 times more easily than ice. The outside of the ice, which is wetter, may be affected, but the entire ice cube will make it through relatively unscathed. Cool, right?

Notes

molecule 分子 / **intact** 無傷の / **airtight** 気密の / **vapor** 蒸気 / **thermal conduction** 熱伝導 / **lumpy** ごつごつした，塊の / **granular** 粉状の / **sterilize** 殺菌する / **intense heat** 高熱 / **liquid** 液体の / **unscathed** 無傷で

T/F Questions

次の英文が本文の内容と一致する場合は T、一致しない場合は F を記入しましょう。

1. [   ] The use of the microwave oven leads to all kinds of different results.

2. [   ] In a microwave oven, microwaves cause water molecules to vibrate slowly.

3. [   ] Metallic objects such as aluminum foil should not be put in a microwave oven.

4. [   ] Heating a wet sponge in a microwave is a good way to make it softer.

5. [   ] Water is heated approximately 800 times more easily than ice.

57

次の英文パッセージは本文を要約したものです。音声を聞いて空所を埋めましょう。

The way microwave ovens work is rather simple. Microwaves cause water molecules in the food or beverage to (1.   ) rapidly, resulting in a rise in the total temperature of the object.

This appliance can be used for purposes other than just (2.   ) something to eat. For example, a mistakenly placed postage stamp can be taken off by (3.   ) the stamp and heating it in a microwave for 20 seconds.

Generally speaking, heating ice makes it (4.   ); however, if we put it in a microwave oven, it is not affected. (5.   ) put, ice won't melt. This is because ice is about 8,000 times more difficult to heat than water. Water molecules in ice almost never vibrate.

TIPS

電子レンジの雑学２つ
●肉まんやあんまんを電子レンジで温めないのはなぜか
　肉まんやあんまんは、コンビニでは専用のケースで温めています。そのケースは蒸気で蒸すようにできており、生地がたっぷりと水蒸気を含むので、温かい状態を保てるのです。電子レンジでは、温めても生地の表面から水蒸気が放出され、すぐに冷めてしまうのです。
●電子レンジにはすごい殺菌力がある
　温度が上がるから殺菌力があるのではなく、そもそも電磁波が細菌の細胞をやっつけるのです。２分間電子レンジにかけると、たいていの食中毒の原因菌を死滅させることができます。水分がないものや金属は電子レンジにかけないようにしましょう。爆発する危険性があります。

UNIT 10   *Ice, Pet Cats, Stamps, and Microwave Ovens*

Grammar Check

次の英文の (　) 内の語 (句) のうち正しい方を選びましょう。

1. People have tried (use / using) microwaves for a variety of purposes.

2. Electric waves interact with water molecules (caused / causing) them to vibrate rapidly.

3. Eggs may explode due to vapors (is / being) unable to escape if the temperature rises.

4. A microwave oven is useful (to take / taking) off postage stamps placed by mistake.

5. (Heat / Heating) a sponge in a microwave is a good way to sterilize it.

6. It is better to avoid (to put / putting) sausages in a microwave, since they may explode.

7. Nancy hopes (to become / becoming) a physicist, who specializes in electromagnetics.

8. I couldn't get him to stop (to smoke / smoking); it seems to have been hard for him.

9. I am ashamed of (being / having been) late for the meeting yesterday.

10. I insisted on her (no / not) meeting him, because he is said to be a swindler.

一口文法　　**動名詞**

動名詞は、ある動詞が名詞として機能する形を指す。形であるから「品詞」ではない。動名詞の基本形式は、doing である。

(a) 意味上の主語は、所有格で表すのが原則：his eating it / Mary's sleeping in bed
　　ただし、前置詞の後は所有格ではなく目的格を用いるのが普通。
　　→ due to vapors being unable to do ~

(b) 否定は前に not を付ける。意味上の主語があれば、その直後に not を置く。
　　→ his not eating it （彼がそれを食べないこと）

(c) 完了形は having done の形にする。
　　→ Mary's not having slept in bed （メアリーがベッドで眠らなかったこと）
　　　※上記の例は、意味上の主語、否定、完了形をすべて合わせたもの。

59

Writing Expressions

次の英文の (　　) 内の単語を並べ替えて、英文を完成させましょう。

1. この話が本当かどうかは別として、非常に重要なことを教えてくれている。
   Whether (is / not / or / story / this / true), it teaches something very important.

   _____

2. 毎日の睡眠時間が短いのは決して良いことではない。
   It (a / idea / is / good / never / to) sleep for only a short period of time every night.

   _____

3. 食物繊維をしっかりとることは便秘解消には良い方法である。
   An increased intake of dietary fibers (a / eliminate / good / is / to / way) constipation.

   _____

4. さて、ここで考えるべきことがあります。ストレスとはそもそも何ですか。
   (consider / here / is / now / something / to) – what is stress all about?

   _____

5. 電子レンジでは、氷を暖めるのが水よりも約8000倍困難である。
   In a microwave, ice is (about / harder / heated / than / times / 8,000) water.

   _____

Discussion Topics

次の質問に答えることをきっかけとして、英語で話し合いましょう。

1. What electric appliance do you like best? And why?

   _____

2. What dish do you usually eat when you eat out? What is your favorite food and why?

   _____

The Unknown Effects of Tatami

畳は、大和民族の生活の知恵が生み出した誇るべき住文化です。しかし、住宅の洋風化が進み、畳のある和室が１部屋あるかないかの現代の家。畳の原材料となるイグサの産地では、需要が以前と比べて７〜８割も減ったそうです。しかし畳には、まだまだ知られていない魅力がたくさんあります。この章ではそんな畳の魅力を学びましょう。

Vocabulary Check

次の単語の定義を下の [a] 〜 [h] から選びましょう。

(1) material (　　)　　(2) layer (　　)　　(3) occasion (　　)
(4) subtle (　　)　　(5) serenity (　　)　　(6) property (　　)
(7) adaptability (　　)　(8) proof (　　)

[a] the act of finding or testing the truth of something
[b] a substance from which things can be made or with which things can be done
[c] a time at which something is or may be done
[d] a relatively thin sheet-like substance lying over or under another
[e] the ability to change to fit different circumstances
[f] the state of being peaceful and calm
[g] not easily noticed because of delicateness or slightness
[h] basic quality that is shared by all members of the same category

Reading

Tatami is a kind of mat developed in Japan used traditionally as a flooring material. The direct translation of the word "tatami" is "fold." Therefore, the word originally referred to any carpet-like flooring material which could be used by folding it several times.

In fact, tatami was used in several layers where people sat or lay down, though at present tatami mats are spread out to cover a room. Moreover, in the past, tatami mats were stored by stacking them one on top of the other, often for use at festivals or on other special occasions.

There are three reasons why tatami is superior to simple flooring. First, it makes little noise when stepped on. The subtle thudding sound made while walking on a mat adds to a feeling of serenity in the room. This particular sound is related to the acoustic absorption properties of tatami. Tatami mats are made of rice straw, a woven material that has very good sound-absorbing properties. People one floor down in an apartment or house will be oblivious to the activity upstairs if tatami is used.

Secondly, tatami is well suited to the muggy climate of Japan. A few of the reasons why tatami is comfortable include its soft elasticity, superior moisture releasing properties, and its hygroscopicity. This means that the temperature control function of tatami is excellent; to be more specific, it absorbs moisture during the rainy season, when humidity is very high, and releases it during the drier winter season. This adaptability ensures that Japanese can enjoy a certain level of comfort at home no matter the season. The way tatami adjusts to temperature and humidity is due to the structure of the rush and straw used in its construction.

Finally, tatami is good for health. The reason is due to the fragrant smell given off by the tatami. Its enticing smell has a sedative effect like one would

UNIT 11   *The Unknown Effects of Tatami*

experience during a therapeutic walk in the forest. Being in a tatami-matted room can make you feel as if you are surrounded by nature. Taking in its fresh scent can result in bodily and spiritual relaxation.

Japanese have become so accustomed to the benefits of tatami that they sometimes overlook them in favor of newer types of tatami. Recent developments 5 have led to synthesized tatami that doesn't lose its freshness and color as easily. They are also lighter than the traditional tatami. However, synthetic tatami doesn't breathe well and is fragile. This is proof of the accuracy of the adage, "if it ain't broke, don't fix it."

Notes

stack 積み重ねる / **thudding sound** 鈍い（衝撃）音 / **acoustic** 音響上の / **absorption** 吸収すること / **oblivious** 気づかない / **muggy** 蒸し暑い / **elasticity** 弾力性 / **hygroscopicity** 吸湿性 / **rush** イグサ / **enticing** 魅惑的な / **synthesize** 合成する / **adage** ことわざ

❀ · · ❀ · · ❀ · · ❀ · · ❀ · · ❀ · · ❀ · · ❀ · · ❀ · · ❀ · · ❀

T/F Questions

次の英文が本文の内容と一致する場合は T、一致しない場合は F を記入しましょう。

1. [   ] Tatami is a kind of mat developed in China.

2. [   ] Tatami mats were spread out to cover a room where people sat or lay down in ancient times.

3. [   ] Tatami has very good sound-absorbing properties, so it can shut out most sound.

4. [   ] Tatami absorbs moisture during the winter season, and releases it during the rainy season.

5. [   ] Tatami has a calming effect and its scent can result in bodily and spiritual relaxation.

63

次の英文パッセージは本文を要約したものです。音声を聞いて空所を埋めましょう。

There are three reasons why tatami, a traditional Japanese flooring material, is (1.　　　　　　) to simple flooring.

First, it makes almost no noise when walked on, since it (2.　　　　　) sound very effectively. Therefore, people living in an apartment are (3.　　　　　　) of the activity going on upstairs when tatami is used.

Secondly, it is suitable for the hot and humid climate of Japan. Tatami absorbs moisture during the rainy season and (4.　　　　　) it during the drier season, which results in greater comfort.

Lastly, it has a positive effect on health. Taking in the (5.　　　　　) smell given off by tatami allows people to relax physically and spiritually.

TIPS

畳のへりを踏んではいけない理由

　畳の文化は平安時代にさかのぼりますが、この時代の名残なのです。畳のへりを染める染料に植物を使用していたので、ここを踏むと染料が落ちてしまうことがありました。また、素材には麻が使用され、これは耐久性が低く、擦り切れてしまう危険性がありました。

　畳は平安時代には大変貴重なぜいたく品だったこともあり、きれいに使うことがマナーだったのです。その名残が「縁を踏んではいけない」ということにつながっているのです。

Grammar Check

次の英文の（　）内の語（句）のうち正しい方を選びましょう。

1. Tatami was used in (several / plenty) layers where people sat or lay down.
2. There are (three / the three) reasons why tatami is superior to simple flooring.
3. Tatami makes (few / little) noise when it is stepped on.
4. (Few / A few) of the reasons why tatami is good include elasticity and hygroscopicity.
5. (No / Not) matter the reason, that is not something that can be allowed.
6. Tatami mats are made (of / into) rice straw, or a sound-absorbing woven material.
7. A fragrant smell is given (over / off) by the tatami, so it enhances our health.
8. Japanese have become used (with / to) the benefits of tatami.
9. Being in a tatami-(matting / matted) room makes us feel really at home.
10. Recent developments have led to (synthesize / synthesized) tatami that doesn't lose its freshness and color.

一口文法　数量詞について

名詞は可算名詞と不可算名詞に分けることができる。これに対応し、その名詞を修飾する数量詞が「多・少」を表す場合に数量詞が異なる。

	すべての	多くの	中間の数量	少ない	ない
数	all	many	some	few	no
量	all	much	some	little	no

注1：不定冠詞の有無の違い
　　a few や a little は肯定的（少しはある）で、few や little は否定的（ほとんどない）。
　　→ There are few people there.（そこには人がほとんどいない）
　　　　We found a little water in the bottle.（そのボトルに少し水があった）

注2：little は可算名詞について「小さな」を表す場合は、普通の形容詞。
　　a little wine（少量のワイン）[数量詞] / a little boy（小さな少年）[形容詞]

Writing Expressions

次の英文の（　　）内の単語を並べ替えて、英文を完成させましょう。

1. 五重塔は鳥居より耐震性の点で優れている。
   A five-storied pagoda (a / gate / is / superior / to / Torii) due to it being quakeproof.

   _____

2. 私たちがくすぐられたときに笑うということは、自己防衛の本能と関係がある。
   The fact we (is / laugh / related / tickled / to / when) a self-defense instinct.

   _____

3. マグネシウムの摂取は足がつるのを避けるのによく適している。
   The intake of magnesium is (of / prevention / suited / the / to / well) calf cramps.

   _____

4. ご都合に合わせることができなくて申し訳ございません。
   I am sorry I could not (a / adjust / convenient / for / time / to) you.

   _____

5. 日本人の中には、正座するのに慣れている人もいる。
   Some Japanese (accustomed / are / sitting / their / to / with) legs bent beneath them.

   _____

Discussion Topics

次の質問に答えることをきっかけとして、英語で話し合いましょう。

1. Which room do you like better, a Japanese tatami-matted room or a Western-style room? And why?

   _____

2. In which room of a house do you feel most comfortable? And why?

   _____

Voice Recognition Sounds Great for Security

暗証番号やパスワードは忘れてしまうと、本人でも認証ができなくなります。そこで、近年、指紋認証、虹彩認証、さらには静脈認証などの利用が増えつつあります。最近では、声による生体認証としての音声認証が注目されています。風邪を引いて声が変わっても大丈夫なのでしょうか。

Vocabulary Check

次の単語の定義を下の [a] ～ [h] から選びましょう。

(1) victim (　　)　　(2) cybercrime (　　)　　(3) identity (　　)
(4) authentication (　　)　　(5) verify (　　)　　(6) acoustic (　　)
(7) digitize (　　)　　(8) security (　　)

[a] relating to sound or hearing
[b] a person's concept of who they are
[c] someone who has suffered loss by being tricked or swindled
[d] illegal acts or activities committed via computers over the Internet
[e] to convert something into a form that can be processed or stored by a computer
[f] measures of protecting data to ensure that only authorized persons can have access to it
[g] to confirm or check that a thing is true, genuine or valid
[h] the action or process of proving or confirming that something or someone is true, genuine or valid

Have you ever lost your keys or forgotten your PIN (Personal Identification Number) code or password and been denied access to buildings or digital devices? Do you worry you will be a victim of cybercrimes such as web spoofing or identity theft? A convenient, safe, and viable solution to these problems is biometric authentication. Biometric authentication systems draw upon personal physical characteristics and biological traits to verify and authenticate an individual. Currently available image-driven biometric technologies include facial recognition, fingerprint scanning, iris/retina scanning, vein recognition, and hand shape recognition. In addition, voice biometrics, based on the acoustic properties of the human voice, is gaining in prominence due to its convenience and versatility.

How does it work? A voiceprint, or a graphic representation of a person's voice, digitizes the acoustic features of the speaker and can be used to legitimize his or her identity. Like fingerprints, no two voiceprints are alike. In voice biometrics, a vocal sample is converted into a voiceprint and submitted to a verification process by comparing it with a pre-registered "reference voiceprint" stored in the database. It is only when the two voiceprints are successfully matched that the identity claim is accepted.

In addition to its function as a security-enhancing tool, applications of voice biometrics are far-reaching and promising in the following areas: criminal identification in forensic investigations, spoof-preventions for monetary transactions, AI assistance, and much more. Broadly speaking, voice recognition is well-suited to any individual who wishes to operate devices or input commands hands-free.

Although a variety of products that use this technology are commercially available, voice biometrics is by no means foolproof. There are both internal and external factors that can cause problems. The variability in a speaker's

UNIT 12 *Voice Recognition Sounds Great for Security*

voice due to emotion, physical conditions, and biological changes over time is troublesome.   A poor-quality microphone or background noise can also lead to undesirable results.   A major challenge is getting the system to recognize one particular voice among many, something humans can do effortlessly.

It is always better to be safe than sorry.   Future trends indicate that voice biometrics will be used in tandem with other forms of biometric recognition technologies.   The use of multiple sources of biometrics is bound to bolster security.

> ### Notes
> **PIN code** 暗証番号 / **web spoofing** ウェブサイトのなりすまし / **viable** 実行可能な / **biometric authentication** 生体認証 / **draw upon** 利用する / **retina** 網膜 / **vein** 静脈 / **voice biometrics** 音声認証 / **gain in prominence** 目立ってくる；注目されるようにな る / **versatility** 多用途性 / **legitimize** 正当化する / **far-reaching** 広範囲に及ぶ / **forensic investigation** 法医学検査 / **foolproof** 絶対確実な，間違えようのない / **in tandem with** 〜と並行して / **bolster** 強化する

T/F Questions

次の英文が本文の内容と一致する場合は T、一致しない場合は F を記入しましょう。

1. [   ] Biometric authentication can provide a convenient and safe solution to cybercrimes such as identity theft.

2. [   ] Currently, voice recognition is more frequently used than facial recognition because of its convenience and simplicity.

3. [   ] Fingerprint recognition is superior to voiceprint recognition because of cost effectiveness.

4. [   ] The performance of a voice biometrics system may not be affected by the variability of human speech sounds.

5. [   ] The combined use of multi-biometrics sources can enhance the performance of personal authentication technologies.

次の英文パッセージは本文を要約したものです。音声を聞いて空所を埋めましょう。

Biometric authentication, drawing upon personal physical characteristics and biological traits, can (1.   ) as an alternative method of identification. Besides image-based biometric technologies, audio-based voice biometrics, based on the acoustic properties of the human voice, is increasingly (2.   ) in prominence, thanks to its convenience and versatility.

How can the speaker's identity be legitimized? A vocal sample is (3.   ) into a voiceprint, which is to be matched against a pre-registered "reference voiceprint" template. Only when the two voiceprints prove to be identical can the identity claim be accepted.

Possible applications of voice biometrics are manifold, including security, fraud prevention, or monitoring. However, voice recognition is not (4.   )-free. Major challenges concern the variability of a speaker's vocal characteristics performance-degrading recording equipment and noisy environments. Therefore, it would be highly (5.   ) to use voice biometrics in combination with other types of identity verifiers.

TIPS

男性はなぜ声変わりをするのか？

人間が二足歩行をするようになって、声帯が広がり、言語を操るのに効果的な喉になったといわれています。

男性は思春期には、さらに声帯が伸び、声が低くなります。男性の声変わりの理由は、女性に対するアピールになっているというのが、生物学的な見解です。声の高い男性よりも、低い男性の方が、女性にもてるというわけです。声が低い方が落ち着いていて、信頼できそうだと感じるという実験結果があります。

UNIT 12 *Voice Recognition Sounds Great for Security*

● Grammar Check

次の英文の (   ) 内の語 (句) のうち自然な方を選びましょう。

1. (It / There) is only when the two voiceprints are matched that the claim is accepted.

2. It is voice recognition (is / that is) well-suited to those who wish to do so hands-free.

3. What (is / is it) that you have been searching for for the past 10 years?

4. (What / There) seems to be more important is that we solve the problem immediately.

5. It was very (elegantly / surprisingly) that Lucy ate her lunch.

6. Having a poor-quality microphone leads to (desirable / undesirable) results.

7. Anything (comprehensible / incomprehensible) interests him; he is full of curiosity.

8. Avitaminosis is the state of (lack / lacking) some vitamins.

9. The town mayor ceremoniously (uncovered / discovered) the new monument in the park.

10. Humans tend to choose something they can do (with effort / effortlessly). Simply, they like to do anything with ease.

一口文法　強調構文の意味と意義

　一般に英文は旧情報から新情報へと情報が流れる。つまり、英文の後ろが言いたいこと（＝強調されること）となる。強調構文は、強調したいものを前に持ってくる構文である。ここに、強調構文の意義が存在する。

　John loves Mary. の一般的な解釈は、Mary が新情報なので、「John は（Lucy や Nancy ではなく）Mary を愛している」という意味となり、これを強調構文で表すと、It is Mary that John loves.（= John が愛しているのは Mary だ）となる。

　先の文 John loves Mary. において、John を新情報にして「（Tom や Bob ではなく）John が Mary を愛している」という意味になるようにする方法は、It is John that loves Mary.（= Mary を愛しているのは John だ）という強調構文のほか、John loves Mary. のままで John に強勢を置いて発音する方法がある。

71

Writing Expressions

次の英文の (　) 内の単語を並べ替えて、英文を完成させましょう。

1. 言語を分類するのに、言語学者は動詞の位置の情報を利用することが多い。
   To classify languages, linguists often (about / draw / information / location / the / upon) of their verbs.

   _____

2. 声紋認証はその利便性と多用途性から、ますます人気が高まっている。
   Voice authentication (due / gaining / in / increasingly / is / prominence) to its convenience and versatility.

   _____

3. 人それぞれの好みに合うように開発された入手可能な商品は、実に色々ある。
   There are a (available / of / products / that / variety / wide) have been developed for individual tastes.

   _____

4. 星を研究する自然科学である天文学は、宇宙を研究する宇宙論の1分野では決して ないが、この2つの科学は深く関係し合っている。
   Astronomy, a natural science involving the study of stars, is (by / cosmology / means / no / of / part) which studies the universe, though the two sciences are deeply related.

   _____

5. 十分なリコピンの摂取、例えば、トマトを1週間に7個より多く食べるなどする と、がんの予防効果が高まるのは間違いない。
   A sufficient intake of lycopene, such as eating more than seven tomatoes a week, is (bound / effect / increase / its / preventive / to) on cancer.

   _____

Discussion Topics

次の質問に答えることをきっかけとして、英語で話し合いましょう。

1. Would you prefer a PIN or password to biometric authentication? Why?

   _____

2. Which type of biometrics would you prefer to use and why?

   _____

Will Space Exploration Unlock the Secrets of the Universe?

宇宙は謎に満ちています。宇宙の果てはどうなっているのでしょうか。ビッグバンの前はどうなっていたのでしょうか。知的生命体は地球外にいるのでしょうか。私たちの太陽系に生命体は存在しているのでしょうか。あるいは、かつて存在していたのでしょうか…本章では宇宙について思いをはせます。

Vocabulary Check

次の単語の定義を下の [a] 〜 [h] から選びましょう。

(1) satellite (　)　　(2) orbit (　)　　(3) astronomer (　)
(4) candidate (　)　(5) prerequisite (　)　(6) compound (　)
(7) generate (　)　　(8) unlock (　)

[a] to move around a moon or planet
[b] to provide a key to the secrets of something or someone
[c] a substance produced by combining two or more chemical elements
[d] something required to satisfy a prior condition
[e] to produce something by means of a physical, chemical, or electronic process
[f] a person or thing regarded as suitable for a position or classification
[g] a scientist who specializes in studying stars, planets, and other celestial objects
[h] a celestial body that revolves around a planet or minor planet

Reading

You may think our moon is something special, considering the way we refer to it as *the* moon. However, our solar system contains many of these natural satellites, with some planets having quite a large number of them. For example, as many as 67 or 69 confirmed moons reportedly orbit Jupiter, the largest planet in our solar system. Of them, Europa, the fourth largest, was discovered by the world-renowned astronomer, Galileo, as early as 1610. This Jovian moon, covered by an icy crust, has been catching astronomers' attention as a strong candidate for its potential to sustain life.

The hunt for signs of past and present life in the solar system has been a motivating factor of space exploration. Astronomers have made some inroads into this area with their study of Europa; space missions have provided convincing evidence of the prerequisite conditions for hosting life.

One study indicates the possibility that beneath Europa's icy crust lies an ocean of liquid water and a rocky seafloor. Liquid water is the most fundamental life-sustaining compound for planetary habitation. Tidal forces resulting from Jupiter's gravitational pull generates internal heat, which theoretically keeps the subsurface ocean from freezing. In addition, the suspected rocky seabed possibly supplies the chemical nutrients that are conducive to the survival of living things.

From spacecraft observations, Europa's icy surface is repeatedly exposed to intense radiation from Jupiter, yielding chemical reactions. Through this process, the hydrogen and oxygen from the water and ice can combine with other materials from Europa's surface to produce a host of chemical compounds like free oxygen (O_2), hydrogen peroxide (H_2O_2), carbon dioxide (CO_2), and sulfur dioxide (SO_2). These compounds could serve as indispensable sources of chemical energy for microbes.

UNIT 13   *Will Space Exploration Unlock the Secrets of the Universe?*

The existence of a subsurface ocean on Europa, while strongly suspected, has not yet been scientifically proven. Meanwhile, to date, space exploration missions have informed us that Jupiter-like planets are common, and many could have Europa-like icy moons, and thus, life-bearing environments. This awareness has led us to speculate whether habitable environments exist beyond 5 Earth. We look forward to good tidings from future space explorers who may hold the key to unlocking the mystery of the universe in their exciting journeys.

Notes

Jovian 木星の / **make some inroads into** 〜に進出する・挑む / **host life** 生命体を育む / **gravitational** 重力の，引力の / **conducive to** 〜を促す / **hydrogen peroxide** 過酸化水素 / **sulfur dioxide** 二酸化硫黄 / **microbe** 微生物 / **good tidings** 良い知らせ (吉報)

T/F Questions

次の英文が本文の内容と一致する場合は T、一致しない場合は F を記入しましょう。

1. [　　] Jupiter is the fourth largest moon in the solar system.

2. [　　] Galileo discovered living things on Europa as early as the 17th century.

3. [　　] An ocean of salty water flowing under the icy surface of Europa, if found, would provide decisive evidence for the existence of life.

4. [　　] Chemical compounds found on the surface of Europa turned out to be useless for the survival of microbes.

5. [　　] Space exploration missions have suggested that life-bearing environments are likely to be found not only on Europa but on other planets and their moons in the solar system.

 **Summary Listening**

次の英文パッセージは本文を要約したものです。音声を聞いて空所を埋めましょう。

　　Our journeys to outer space have been strongly (1.　　　　　) by our interest in searching for signs of extraterrestrial life. In this regard, since its discovery by Galileo, icy Europa, the fourth-largest moon that orbits Jupiter, has been drawing worldwide attention as a strong (2.　　　　　) for hosting life beyond Earth. Several missions to this moon have indicated the possibility of a subterranean ocean of salty water with a rocky seabed, both of (3.　　　　　) presumably provide the fundamental preconditions to sustain life: water and chemical nutrients.

　　Space exploration missions have also found that life-bearing environments are not limited to Europa, thus greatly (4.　　　　　) our speculation on the existence of extraterrestrial life elsewhere in our solar system. We look forward to new discoveries that may (5.　　　　　) the mysteries of the universe.

TIPS

宇宙に存在する不思議な星
　VFTS102という星は高速回転しています。なんと時速160万ｋｍという想像を絶する速さです。5つから成るラブジョイ彗星（すいせい）の1つに、ワインをまき散らす星があり、1秒間にワインボトル500本分のワインを放射しています。HD189733bという星は、時速7,000ｋｍの猛烈な暴風の中、ガラスの雨が降っていると考えられています。その時の暴風の温度は1,000度以上になります。

UNIT 13   *Will Space Exploration Unlock the Secrets of the Universe?*

Grammar Check

次の英文の（　）内の語（句）のうち正しい方を選びましょう。

1. As (many / much) as 67 or 69 confirmed moons reportedly orbit Jupiter.

2. Jupiter is the (larger / largest) planet in our solar system.

3. Europa, which was discovered by Galileo, is Jupiter's (four / fourth) largest moon.

4. Liquid water is the (most / much) fundamental compound for planetary habitation.

5. He has (three / third) times as many books in his study as his father.

6. The existence of an ocean on Europa (have / has) not yet scientifically proven.

7. Space exploration missions (are / have) informed us that Jupiter-like planets are common.

8. Man has always been (tried / trying) to peer into the unknown to seek for the truth.

9. That was the first time they (have / had) ever eaten Turkish food.

10. Ms. Jackson was a widow. Her husband (died / had died) eight years ago.

一口文法　　**比較**

　形容詞や副詞には原級、比較級、最上級の３つの形がある。典型的な構造と共に示すと次のようになる。副詞の最上級の the は省略されることが多い。

	単語	原級	比較級	最上級
形容詞	large useful	as large as as useful as	larger than more useful than	the largest of/in the most useful of/in
副詞	fast seriously	as fast as as seriously as	faster than more seriously than	(the) fastest of (the) most seriously of

　　注１：最上級に the が付かない場合は、他者と比べず、主語の状況に触れている。
　　　　　→ She looks happiest when she studies.
　　　　　（彼女は勉強している時が最も幸せそうだ）
　　注２：倍数比較の構文は次の通り。
　　　　　(a)「〜と比べて X 倍…だ」→ X times as … as 〜
　　　　　(b)「〜と比べて X 倍の数/量の Y」→ X times as many/much Y as 〜
　　　　　(c)「〜の X 倍の Y の Z」→ a Z X times the Y of 〜
　　　　　　　例：「太陽の 1000 倍の質量の星」→ a star 1000 times the mass of
　　　　　　　　　the sun
　　注３：「〜も」を表す表現：数の場合は as many as、量の場合は as much as を用いる。
　　　　　→ as many as 10 pears（梨 10 個も）/ as much as 100 km（100km も）
　　注４：「n 番目に…な X」は nth …est X となる。
　　　　　→ the fourth largest moon（4 番目に大きい衛星）

77

Writing Expressions

次の英文の（　　）内の単語を並べ替えて、英文を完成させましょう。

1. 2乗してマイナス1となる数字を虚数と呼ぶ。
   We refer to the number (as / is / minus / one / square / whose) an imaginary number.

   _____

2. 量子力学の専門家の中には、生まれ変わりの謎に迫ろうとする人たちがすでにいる。
   Some experts in quantum mechanics (inroads / into / made / mystery / some / the) of reincarnation.

   _____

3. 十分に睡眠を取れば、副交感神経が優位になり、血液循環の正常化を促進する。
   A sufficient amount of sleep will be (blood / circulation / conducive / due / normal / to) to its causing parasympathetic dominance.

   _____

4. 過酸化水素などの化合物は、微生物にとって不可欠な化学エネルギーの源となるだろう。
   Compounds like hydrogen peroxide could (as / chemical / indispensable / of / serve / sources) energy for microbes.

   _____

5. 量子力学は死後の世界を解き明かす鍵を握っているかもしれないと主張する科学者たちがいる。
   Some scientists insist that quantum mechanics (hold / key / may / the / to / unlocking) the mystery of the next world.

   _____

Discussion Topics

次の質問に答えることをきっかけとして、英語で話し合いましょう。

1. Which do you like better, the sun or the moon? And why?

   _____

2. Do you believe in the existence of UFOs? Do you think intelligent life exists on some planets in the universe?

   _____

Twinkle, Twinkle Little Star– How I Wonder How Bright You Are!

星はキラキラ輝いています。太陽はギラギラと、私たちに恵みの光と熱を与えてくれています。他の恒星に比べ、太陽は私たちに近いところにあるので、すごくまぶしいのですが、他の星と同じような位置にあれば、太陽もキラキラと表現することになるのでしょう。本章では、星の明るさについて掘り下げます。

 Vocabulary Check

次の単語の定義を下の [a] 〜 [h] から選びましょう。

(1) radiant (　　) (2) classify (　　) (3) dim (　　)
(4) quantify (　　) (5) perceive (　　) (6) intrinsic (　　)
(7) radius (　　) (8) static (　　)

[a] shining brightly
[b] not clearly seen, faint
[c] not moving, changing, or progressing
[d] the distance from the center to the outside edge of a circle
[e] to calculate something to represent or express it in numbers
[f] to view or interpret something or someone in a particular way
[g] to arrange or organize things into groups according to their similar characteristics
[h] relating to its basic nature or character of something, not dependent on external conditions

When gazing at the night sky, you may notice that some stars look more radiant than others. The concept of ranking the brightness of stars started as early as over 2,000 years ago, when the Greek astronomer Hipparchus classified stars in terms of how bright they appear. The brightest stars were classified as magnitude 1, the next brightest as magnitude 2, etc., down to the dimmest stars visible as magnitude 6. His magnitude scale was later extended to much brighter and fainter stars and quantified into a logarithmic scale, with each magnitude representing a brightness change of 2.5 units from the subsequent step.

Today's astronomers commonly employ two indexes: apparent magnitude, i.e., how bright a star is perceived to be when viewed from Earth and absolute magnitude, i.e., how bright a star appears at a standard distance of 32.6 light-years, or 10 parsecs. The calculation unit, a light-year, is the distance that light can travel in one year. Light travels at a speed of about 300,000 kilometers per second. That means in one year, it can travel about 10 trillion kilometers. The parsec is roughly equal to 3.3 light-years and is commonly used by astronomers.

Apparent magnitude is relatively simple to understand. The limitation, however, is its dependence on the distance of the object from the observer. For example, Venus appears brighter than any star, but this brightness is due to its closeness to Earth.

In contrast, absolute magnitude factors out the distance parameters. This measurement is defined as the apparent magnitude an object would have if it were located 10 parsecs from Earth. Therefore, for example, the apparent magnitude of the sun, the brightest celestial object observable from Earth, stands at -26.7. However, if the sun were 10 parsecs away, its magnitude would be +4.7. It's important to note that the lower an object falls on the brightness scale, the brighter the celestial object is.

UNIT 14   *Twinkle, Twinkle Little Star– How I Wonder How Bright You Are!*

Another way to measure brightness is by luminosity, which takes into account intrinsic stellar brightness. Luminosity refers to the amount of energy, or light, that a star radiates from its surface, measured in watts using solar luminosity as a reference unit. A star's luminosity depends on its radius and surface temperature. If the radius is equal, a hotter star is more luminous, and   5 if the temperature is equal, a bigger star is more luminous.

However, a star's luminosity is not static and can change over time. The North Star, or Polaris, for example, could have been as much as 4.6 times brighter in ancient times. A study pointed out that although the star dimmed over the past few decades, it drastically brightened again. Indeed, the universe   10 is a treasure trove of mysteries, far beyond our imagination.

> **Notes**
>
> **Hipparchus** ヒッパルコス（紀元前 2 世紀の天文学者：初めて星図を作成し三角法を発明したといわれる）/ **logarithmic** 対数の / **parsec** パーセク (3.26 光年に当たる天体の距離を表す単位) / **factor out...** …の要因を考慮に入れない / **the distance parameters** 距離の要因（変数）/ **celestial** 天の，天体の / **luminosity** 光度 / **stellar** 星の / **treasure trove** 宝庫；貴重な発見

⬤ T/F Questions

次の英文が本文の内容と一致する場合は T、一致しない場合は F を記入しましょう。

1. [   ] The idea of the brightness ranking of stars can be traced back to Roman times.

2. [   ] The brighter the star is, the higher on the brightness scale.

3. [   ] One light-year is equal to 3.3 trillion kilometers.

4. [   ] Because of its closeness to Earth, Venus is perceived to be more radiant than any star.

5. [   ] A star's luminosity is constant and is not likely to change in the future.

次の英文パッセージは本文を要約したものです。音声を聞いて空所を埋めましょう。

The idea of ranking a star's brightness was (1.   ) by a Greek astronomer as early as over 2,000 years ago. The 6-point measurement scale was later converted into a logarithmic scale. Using this system, the lower the star is posited on the scale, the brighter it is (2.   ) to be.

Currently there are three measures of star brightness. The first one, apparent magnitude, indicates how bright a star appears to be when viewed from Earth. The second type, absolute magnitude, factors out the distance parameters and measures by imagining how bright stellar objects would (3.   ) if they were placed all at a standard distance of 32.6 light years, or ten parsecs. The last measure is luminosity, which (4.   ) the intrinsic brightness of a star, or the amount of energy (light) that a star emits from its surface. However, a star's luminosity is not (5.   ), so a luminous star today may be dim in the distant future.

TIPS

星といえば夜、夜といえば睡眠、睡眠といえば電車内

電車内は、バスや船、飛行機よりも眠りにつきやすいですね。特に、座席に座ると眠くなることが多いのですが、これはなぜでしょう。バスや船より揺れが激しくなく、飛行機にはない独特のリズムがあることが、眠気を誘う原因なのでしょう。

しかし、お母さんの胎内の音に電車の走行音がそっくりである点も大きな要因とされています。つまり、自分が生まれる前のお母さんの胎内を無意識に思い出しているということになります。実際に、泣いている赤ちゃんに、胎内と同じ音を聞かせると、赤ちゃんは心地よく感じ、泣きやむことが多いという実験結果があります。

UNIT 14   *Twinkle, Twinkle Little Star– How I Wonder How Bright You Are!*

⬤ Grammar Check

次の英文の (　) 内の語 (句) のうち正しい方を選びましょう。

1. Some stars look (a lot / more) radiant than others.

2. The idea of the brightness ranking of stars started as (early / fast) as 2,000 years ago.

3. The (brighter / brightest) stars were classified as magnitude 1.

4. Venus appears brighter than (any / some) other planet in the solar system.

5. The lower a star falls on the brighter scale, (a brighter / the brighter) it becomes.

6. If the sun (is / were) 100 parsec away, its magnitude would be +4.7.

7. If the temperature (is / were) equal, a bigger star is more luminous.

8. It is likely to be fine today, but if it (will / should) rain, take the clothes in.

9. She would have lost her hearing if the operation (weren't / hadn't) been successful.

10. If Sam had gone to college when he finished high school, he would (be / have been) a junior now.

一口文法　仮定法

　仮定法とは現実とは異なることを仮定する表現形式で、次の 3 つの形式が典型的である。
　(a) 仮定法過去：現在の事実に反することを仮定する
　(b) 仮定法過去完了：過去の事実に反することを仮定する
　(c) 仮定法 should：未来の確実とされることに反することを仮定する
　それぞれの構造式は次の通りである。
　(a)　If S1 were/ 過去形〜 , S2 would V2….
　　　（もし今 S1 が〜であったら S2 は V2 だろうに）
　(b)　If S1 had V1-ed 〜 , S2 would have V2-ed….
　　　（もしあの時 S1 が V1 であったら、S2 は V2 だっただろうに）
　(c)　If S1 should V1 〜 , S2 would/will V2….
　　　（万一、S1 が V1 だったら、S2 は V2 するだろう）
　注 1 : if の省略形は 3 種類
　　(a) Were S1 〜 , …. (b) Had S1 V1-ed 〜 , …. (c) Should S1 V1 〜 , ….
　注 2 : 仮定法過去と仮定法過去完了が組み合わせられる場合がある。
　→ If she had not helped me at that time, I would not be successful now.
　（もしあの時、彼女が私を助けてくれなかったら、今の私の成功はないだろう）

Writing Expressions

次の英文の（　　）内の単語を並べ替えて、英文を完成させましょう。

1. 地震を揺れの大きさの観点から分類することで、震度という概念が生まれた。
   The concept of "shindo" came into being by (classifying / how / in / of / terms / quakes) great the shake is.

   _____

2. 毛は日本の昔の金額の単位の1つで、1毛とは1銭の100分の1に等しい。
   "Mo" is one of the old monetary units under which (a / equal / is / "mo" / one / to) hundredth of one "sen."

   _____

3. ある物体の質量という概念は、その物体の地球上での重さから重力加速度の要素を取り除いたものである。
   The concept of the mass of an object refers to what is gained by (acceleration / factoring / from / gravitational / its / out) weight on earth.

   _____

4. ある文の多義性を客観的に示すには、順列と組み合わせという数学的方程式を考慮に入れることが重要である。
   To objectively indicate the polysemy of a sentence, it is important (account / into / mathematical / take / the / to) equations of permutations and combinations.

   _____

5. ビッグバン以前には何があったのか、これからの宇宙はどうなっていくのかという2つの謎については、今のところ、私たちの想像をはるかに超える。
   Two mysteries, what existed before the Big Bang and in what direction the universe will go, (are / at / beyond / far / imagination / our) present.

   _____

Discussion Topics

次の質問に答えることをきっかけとして、英語で話し合いましょう。

1. Do you like to gaze at stars with the naked eye or through a telescope?

   _____

2. Do you believe in horoscopes? What is your astrological sign?

   _____

A Story of Folding Paper

日本の伝統的遊戯の1つである折り紙の起源は、上級武士の折形（おりがた）礼法にあります。これは和紙で物を包むための礼法ですが、この折形礼法から礼法の部分がなくなって庶民用に発展した遊戯が現在の折り紙です。ところで、紙は何回まで折ることが可能でしょうか。また、折った時の厚さについて、驚くべき事実があります。その事実とは…？

Vocabulary Check

次の単語の定義を下の [a] ～ [h] から選びましょう。

(1) head (　　)　　(2) distribute (　　)　　(3) double (　　)
(4) theoretical (　　)　　(5) impressive (　　)　　(6) proportional (　　)
(7) massive (　　)　　(8) locate (　　)

[a] to give things to a number of people; share something between a number of people
[b] to be going in a particular direction
[c] concerned with scientific principles on which a particular subject is based
[d] to make things or a substance become twice as many or as much
[e] at a constant ratio to something; in the proper relationship to something
[f] causing people feel something is great in size, quality, beauty, etc.
[g] very great in size, amount, or weight
[h] to find the exact position of something or somebody

Reading

We seem to be rapidly headed towards a paperless society; however, teachers continue to distribute paper handouts as materials for their classes. Students take full advantage of the abundance of paper by jotting down what they learn on these handouts or in their notebooks.

Handouts are usually made by photocopying what teachers print out from a file they make, so they are usually made of xerographic paper. Not to get sidetracked, but how many times do you think we can fold such paper? We can manage to fold A4-sized paper six times; however, it is almost impossible to fold it seven times, and impossible to do it eight times. The thickness of most paper is 0.09mm, though there are some types that are thicker than this. Every time we fold it, the thickness will be doubled. If the paper is folded eight times, the theoretical thickness will be 256 times the thickness of the original, due to two to the eighth power being 256, which means it will be 2.304 cm thick. This is a result of the calculation: $0.09 \times 2^8 \div 10$.

This thickness itself is not so impressive but the power needed to fold the paper eight times is unbelievably great. Generally, the force required to firmly fold something that is not broken is proportional to the thickness to the third power. This means the second folding requires eight times the original force required at the time of the first folding ($2^3=8$). According to this calculation, the required power of the seventh folding is 262,144 times greater than the first. This calculation usually applies to the bending of girders; however, it also pertains to the case of paper.

Incidentally, the figure of 86 is not relatively large but if paper is folded 86 times, then theoretically, the thickness will be so massive that it will extend into space past the Andromeda Galaxy, which is located about 2.5 million light years away from Earth. Check out how thick paper can become if folded a certain number of times.

UNIT 15 *A Story of Folding Paper*

22 times: higher than the Eiffel Tower

23 times: taller than the Tokyo Skytree

24 times: greater than the Burj Khalifa, the highest building in the world

26 times: surpasses Mt. Fuji, the highest mountain in Japan

42 times: beyond the distance to the moon   5

51 times: farther than the sun

86 times: far past the distance to the Andromeda Galaxy!

Notes

jot down ちょっと書き留める / **xerographic paper** コピー用紙 / **get sidetracked** 横道にそれる / **two to the eighth power** 2の8乗 / **girder** [建築用語] 桁，大梁 / **pertain to** 〜に関係がある・属する / **Burj Khalifa** ブルジュ・ハリファ

T/F Questions

次の英文が本文の内容と一致する場合は T、一致しない場合は F を記入しましょう。

1. [   ] It is very difficult to fold paper eight times, but it is possible if you try hard.

2. [   ] If you fold paper eight times, the folded paper will be 2.304 cm thick.

3. [   ] The force needed to fold something is proportional to the square of its thickness.

4. [   ] The Milky Way is 2.5 million light-years from Earth.

5. [   ] If paper is folded 51 times, its thickness will exceed the distance to the sun.

87

 **Summary Listening**

次の英文パッセージは本文を要約したものです。音声を聞いて空所を埋めましょう。

　　Realistically speaking, it is impossible for us to (1.　　　　　) any piece of paper more than seven times. If it was possible to fold paper ad infinitum, the results would be surprising. Since paper is usually 0.09mm thick, the (2.　　　　　　　) thickness in meters when paper is folded x number of times will be a result of the (3.　　　　　):$0.09 \times 2^x \div 1000$. The thickness of paper folded 22 times will surpass the (4.　　　　) of the Eiffel Tower. The thickness of paper folded 24 times soars above the highest building in the world, the Burj Khalifa. When folded 42 times, paper will become (5.　　　　　　　) than the distance to the moon. Finally, when paper is folded only 86 times, the thickness will reach the Andromeda Galaxy and beyond!

TIPS

超高層ビル、ブルジュ・ハリファ
　ブルジュ・ハリファは 2018 年現在、世界一高い建物です。このビルは、アラブ首長国連邦のドバイにあり、828.9 m の高さで 206 階建てです。122 階にレストラン、144 階にナイトクラブがありますが、それぞれ世界一高いところに存在するレストランとナイトクラブです。206 階ありますが、160 階以上は機械室となっており、実際は 159 階までしか入れません。1 ～ 39 階はアルマーニホテル、44 ～ 108 階は居住スペース、111 ～ 154 階はオフィス、156 ～ 159 階は通信・放送室となっています。43 階と 76 階のスカイロビーにはプールが備わっています。

UNIT 15   *A Story of Folding Paper*

⬤ Grammar Check

次の英文の (　) 内の語 (句) のうち正しい方を選びましょう。

1. We seem (being / to be) rapidly headed towards a paperless society.

2. (None / Not) to get sidetracked, but how many times can we fold paper?

3. We can manage (to fold / folded) A4-sized paper six times.

4. It is almost impossible for us (to fold / to be folded) paper seven times.

5. The force required (firmly folded / to firmly fold) something is proportional to the thickness to the third power.

6. Do you know how thick paper can become if it (is / will be) folded 42 times?

7. As soon as I (get / would get) an answer to the question, I will let you know.

8. Even if it rains tomorrow, I'll do field work there if my research assistant (will / wants).

9. Why didn't you come down to meet me if you (are / were) upstairs when I visited you?

10. I really want to know when it (rains / will rain) next week. On the day, I will stay home and study hard.

一口文法   不定詞

　　不定詞は、典型的には< to ＋動詞の原形>の形をとる準動詞である。

　　to という要素が暗示するように、未来志向の意味を持つので、未来の事柄を述べる動詞と親和性がある。

　　→ plan to do, decide to do, hope to do, wish to do, want to do など。

　　名詞的用法、形容詞的用法、副詞的用法の３種類がある。

　　(a) 名詞的用法：主語、補語または目的語になる。→ to do…　…すること

　　(b) 形容詞的用法：形容詞として名詞を修飾する。→ N to do…　…するための N

　　(c) 副詞的用法：副詞として動詞を修飾する。→ V ～ to do…　…するために V する

　　　　注１：意味上の主語 S は for で表し、否定は not を to の前に付け、完了形は to have V-ed の形をとる。→ for S not to have V-ed（S が V しなかったこと）

　　　　注２：使役動詞 (let, have, make) や知覚感覚動詞 (see, hear など) の第５文型の文では原形不定詞 (＝ to がない形) が用いられる。→ let me <u>know</u>（私に知らせる）

　　　　注３：to do…の to と do の間に副詞が入る場合がある。

　　　　　　→ to quickly solve ～ （～を即座に解決する）

　　　　　　　　to better understand ～ （～をよりよく理解する）

89

Writing Expressions

次の英文の（　　）内の単語を並べ替えて、英文を完成させましょう。

1. 彼らは天気が良いのを十分に活用してハイキングに行った。
   They (advantage / full / good / of / the / took) weather to go on a hike.

   _____

2. 私はどちらにしようかと迷ったときはいつも、難しい方を選ぶようにしている。
   Every (am / I / in / minds / time / two), I try to choose the more
   challenging option.

   _____

3. 彼は外見上はそれほど印象的ではないが、面白い発想が豊かである。
   He is (appearance / but / impressive / in / not / so) rich in interesting
   ideas.

   _____

4. 速度が一定であれば、進む距離は費やされる時間に比例する。
   If the velocity is constant, the (distance / is / proportional / reached /
   time / to) spent.

   _____

5. 彼女の以前の提案は、現在の問題解決に適用できる。
   Her previous suggestion (apply / can / of / solution / the / to) the
   current problem.

   _____

Discussion Topics

次の質問に答えることをきっかけとして、英語で話し合いましょう。

1. Tell me about any mysterious experience that you have had before.

   _____

2. Is there anything that surprised you most in recent years? Tell me more
   about it.

   _____

Is the Tanabata Story Wrong?

中国の南北朝時代のある書物に「7月7日に牽牛（けんぎゅう）と織り姫が会合する夜」とあり、いわゆる七夕伝説の起源とされています。日本には奈良時代に伝わり、元からあった棚機津女（たなばたつめ）の伝説と習合して、日本の七夕が生まれました。星の一生は長いので、星の身になれば、1年に1度会うのを許されることは、いったいどんな感じなのでしょうか。

Vocabulary Check

次の単語の定義を下の [a] ～ [h] から選びましょう。

(1) expanse (　　) (2) magnitude (　　) (3) volume (　　)
(4) threaten (　　) (5) replace (　　) (6) extremely (　　)
(7) minute (　　) (8) frequently (　　)

[a] the amount of space that something fills; the amount of sound that is produced
[b] often; on many occasions
[c] extremely small; very detailed and careful
[d] the degree to which a star is bright; the degree to which something is large or important
[e] a wide and open space or area of something
[f] to be likely to cause something unpleasant
[g] to be used instead of something or somebody
[h] very great in degree; not ordinary or usual at all

Reading

Each year, on one night during the summer, a star in the constellation of Lyre, Vega, and another star in the constellation of Aquila, Altair, appear in the eastern sky and face each other with the expanse of the Milky Way spreading out between them. The old folk tale of Tanabata has Vega representing a female weaver, and Altair a male cowherder. These lovers are fated to meet but once a year.

The above-mentioned stars and Deneb of the constellation Cygnus form a triangle, which is called the Great Summer Triangle. All three stars are of the first magnitude. Deneb appears the odd one out, but there is a story of Deneb acting as a kind of Cupid for Vega and Altair.

According to legend, on the 7th day of July in a certain year, the rainy weather made it impossible for Vega and Altair to meet by crossing the Milky Way, because the volume of water flowing in the Milky Way increased. Since this meeting was possible only on this day, Deneb stepped in to offer a helping hand.

According to a well-known story, a magpie with open wings bridges the gap between Vega and Altair when the deluge threatens to keep them apart. However, in a variant rendition, Deneb replaces the magpie.

The life of a fixed star is about ten billion years, so this can apply to both Vega and Altair too. If they were living beings, how would they experience one year? Taking the average life span of 80 years into consideration, the period of time stars may experience as one year is the result of the following ratio equation:

$$10{,}000{,}000{,}000 : 80 = 1 : x$$

In this equation, the unit for x is "year," so x will be an extremely small number. For a better understanding, the answer should be calculated in seconds. It is perhaps clearer to look at this in a different way - in this case in terms of y in the following equation:

$$10,000,000,000 : 80 = 365 \times 24 \times 60 \times 60 : y$$

We can find y if we perform the following calculation:

$$y = 80 \times (365 \times 24 \times 60 \times 60) \div 10,000,000,000 = 0.252288$$

In conclusion, the two stars experience a year as only 0.25 second. This span of time is so minute that they may feel that they are meeting each other quite frequently. In fact, they'd probably be tired of looking at each other by now!

Notes

constellation 星座 / **Lyre** 琴座 / **Vega** 織り姫星，ベガ / **Aquila** 鷲座 / **Altair** 牽牛星，アルタイル / **female weaver** 織り姫 / **cowherder** 牛飼い / **Deneb** デネブ / **Cygnus** 白鳥座 / **Great Summer Triangle** 夏の大三角形 (琴座 α 星のベガ・鷲座 α 星のアルタイル・白鳥座 α 星のデネブでできる三角形) [α 星とは 1 つの星座の中で最も明るい星] / **the odd one out** 仲間外れになっているもの / **magpie** [鳥] カササギ / **deluge** 大洪水 / **variant** 別の / **rendition** 解釈

T/F Questions

次の英文が本文の内容と一致する場合は T、一致しない場合は F を記入しましょう。

1. [   ] Altair is a star in the constellation of Lyre.
2. [   ] Deneb serves as a kind of Cupid for Vega and Altair in a certain story.
3. [   ] Vega plays the role of bridging the gap between Deneb and Altair.
4. [   ] The author regards the average human life span as 80 years.
5. [   ] If they were alive, Vega and Altair would experience one year as being far less than 0.25 second.

 **Summary Listening**

次の英文パッセージは本文を要約したものです。音声を聞いて空所を埋めましょう。

　　According to the well-known Tanabata story, Vega and Altair, a mythical couple (1.　　　　　　) by stars, meet once a year. If a person were to have the same lifespan as a star, they might feel a once-a-year meeting is an extraordinarily (2.　　　　　　　) occurrence. The frequency with which one would experience the rendezvous taking place can be calculated by the following formula: 80×(365×24×60×60)÷10,000,000,000. The result of the calculation is a (3.　　　　　　) of second – 0.252288. The meeting would feel as if it were occurring nearly once every 0.25 second. This is because a fixed star lives for 10 billion years, which means the annual meeting will take (4.　　　　　　) ten billion times in a star's lifetime. A human being lives up to about eighty years of age in Japan. If two Japanese people were to meet this way 10 billion times, then the time between two (5.　　　　　　　) meetings would be only about 0.25 second!

TIPS

7月7日にはどんな記念日があるか？

　七夕の織姫の連想から「ゆかたの日」（日本ゆかた連合会が 1981 年に制定）、天の川のイメージから「川の日」（日本の建設省 [現在の国土交通省]）が近代河川制度 100 周年に当たる 1996 年に制定）、そうめんを天の川に見立て「乾麺デー」（全国乾麺協同組合連合会が 1982 年に制定）、年に一度（七夕）の贈り物という連想から「ギフトの日」（全日本ギフト用品協会が 1987 年に制定）などがあります。

UNIT 16   *Is the Tanabata Story Wrong?*

⬤ Grammar Check

次の英文の (　　) 内の語 (句) のうち、自然な方を選びましょう。

1. If the stars were living beings, how (will / would) they experience one year?

2. (Without / But) the sun, no living things would survive.

3. The wise person would know better than (doing / to do) such a thing.

4. I recommend that she (read / reads) the book that I bought last month.

5. What would happen if we (are / were) to lose the secret of making fire?

6. In fact, they would probably be tired of looking (each other / at each other).

7. All the people helped (one another / another one) in the disaster-stricken area.

8. Neither of them uttered a word, but (each / every) seemed to understand the other.

9. John thinks that Mary loves (him / himself), but in fact, he is not sure.

10. We could say that modern technology is not dangerous (in / by) itself.

一口文法　　**相互代名詞・再帰代名詞と人称代名詞の違い**

　相互代名詞は典型的には 2 人の場合の each other や 3 人以上の one another が代表的で、「お互い」を意味する。一方、再帰代名詞は oneself の形で、「〜自身」を意味する。さらに、人称代名詞には、I, we, you, he, she, they とその変化形がある。
　相互代名詞や再帰代名詞は、先行詞（それが指している名詞）が同じ節内に存在することを要求するのに対し、人称代名詞は先行詞が同じ節内に存在しないことを要求する。
　　→○ We think they praised each other. [each other は同節内の they を指せる]
　　　× We think Mary praised each other. [each other は同節内にない we を指せない]
　John thinks Mary loves himself. で himself は Mary を先行詞にできないので、これは非文法的である。
　また John が同一節内にあれば、himself が John を指せるが、同一節内にないので、その解釈もできない。つまりこの文（John thinks Mary loves himself.）は「ジョンはメアリーが自分自身 [= ジョン] のことを愛している」という意味にはならない。
　　→ John killed him. で、人称代名詞 him は同一節内の John を指せない。
　　　だから「ジョンは自殺した」の意味にならない。
　　一方、John thinks Mary loves him. で him は、John が同一節内にないから、John を指すことができるが、先行詞が別の節にないといけないわけではないので、John を指さない場合もある。
　　注：each other は「お互いに」という副詞句ではない。
　　　→お互いに語り合う：○ talk with each other / × talk each other

95

Writing Expressions

次の英文の（　　）内の単語を並べ替えて、英文を完成させましょう。

1. 大雨のために私たちはピクニックに行くことができなかった。
   The heavy rain (for / impossible / it / made / to / us) go on a picnic.

   _____

2. 相互理解が2つの文化の溝を埋めるのに役立つものだ。
   The mutual understanding (between / bridge / gap / serves / the / to)
   the two cultures.

   _____

3. 彼が言ったことを考慮すると、私たちは方針を変えた方がよいだろう。
   (consideration / he / into / said / taking / what), it is better for us to
   change our policy.

   _____

4. より良く理解するためには、それを異なる角度から議論をする必要がある。
   For a better understanding, we need to (a / different / discuss / from / it
   / perspective).

   _____

5. 彼女はあまりに細かな違いにこだわるので、私は少し困った。
   She worried (about / differences / minute / much / so / that) I was a bit
   puzzled.

   _____

Discussion Topics

次の質問に答えることをきっかけとして、英語で話し合いましょう。

1. What annual event do you like best? And why?

   _____

2. How often do you meet your close friend? How about your boyfriend or
   girlfriend?

   _____

How to Use Numbers in Japanese

数を数える時とその数を示す時では、手の形が異なります。例えば、「2」についていえば、日本人は、それを数えている時は、親指と人差し指を折っている状態ですが、人に示す時はVサインをします。また、1～10の昇順と10～1の降順の数え方の微妙な違い、さらに、0を意味する「零」と「ゼロ」の不思議な使い分けが分かりますか。

 Vocabulary Check

次の単語の定義を下の [a] ～ [h] から選びましょう。

(1) pronounce (　) 　 (2) originate (　) 　 (3) vocalize (　)
(4) respectively (　) 　 (5) suffix (　) 　 (6) forecast (　)
(7) precipitation (　) 　 (8) result (　)

[a] to say what one thinks will happen in the future based on information available
[b] in the same order as the things or people already mentioned
[c] a letter or a group of letters added to the end of a word
[d] something that is caused by something else
[e] rain, snow, etc. that falls
[f] to happen or appear for the first time
[g] to say a word with the use of a voice; to use words to express something
[h] to make the sound of a letter or word

Reading

Numbers can be pronounced in two ways in Japanese, one influenced by the Chinese language and the other originating in Japan. The former is *ichi*, *ni*, *san*, *shi*, and so on - the latter is *hi*, *fu*, *mi*, *yo*, etc. For everyday life, counting or vocalizing numbers centers on the former, since this system makes it possible to use numbers greater than ten.

The Chinese-influenced counting system also has three numbers pronounced in two ways: four, seven, and nine. They are pronounced *shi* and *yon*, *shichi* and *nana*, and *ku* and *kyu*, respectively. The different ways to say these numbers can be found when they are counted. Most people say *ichi*, *ni*, *san*, *shi*, *go*, *roku*, *shichi*, *hachi*, *ku*, *ju* when counting up; however, when counting down, it may go *ju*, *kyu*, *hachi*, *nana*, *roku*, *go*, *yon*, *san*, *ni*, *ichi*.

Basically, four, seven, and nine mean the same when they are pronounced differently. However, Japanese has another number that can be said in two ways, which is expressed as zero. That is, zero can be pronounced as "rei" or "zero." There is some significance in that they can be pronounced differently, and in fact, there may be at least two reasons why this number has two ways of being vocalized.

First, if you add a Chinese character referring to time, degree, and the like, it will be pronounced "rei-ji," "rei-do," and so on. Since a Chinese-based suffix is added, "zero" should be read in the Chinese way, not like the English reading of "zero."

Secondly, "rei" connotes a very small amount. One of the typical examples of this is found when forecasting the probability of precipitation. If the chance of rainfall is four percent, then the probability will be expressed as "rei" percent, since the rainfall chance is rounded off to the nearest ten percent. If it is five percent, then ten percent will be the result. This is the reason "rei," which covers more than zero, is used to express figures of precipitation probability.

UNIT 17   *How to Use Numbers in Japanese*

Another example showing that "rei" can mean "very small" is the Japanese phrase "reisai kigyo," meaning a very small company.

On the other hand, "zero" is used to mean complete nothingness, as in the slogan "Gomi Zero Undo," which means "No Garbage Campaign."

As seen in the above explanation, understanding the differences between two similar things is sometimes quite interesting and meaningful.

> **Notes**
>
> **connote** 暗示する / **the probability of precipitation** 降水確率 [=precipitation probability; rainfall chance] / **round off A to B** A を B の概数で表す，A を B に四捨五入する

* · · * · · * · · * · · * · · * · · * · · * · · * · · * · · * · · *

T/F Questions

次の英文が本文の内容と一致する場合は T、一致しない場合は F を記入しましょう。

1. [   ] The Chinese-influenced counting system enables us to count to more than 10.

2. [   ] Five numbers in the Chinese-based system can be pronounced in two ways.

3. [   ] There is a slight difference in usage between "zero" and "rei."

4. [   ] The word "rei" is used to describe figures related to rainfall chance.

5. [   ] The Japanese word "zero" is used to mean a very small company.

99

次の英文パッセージは本文を要約したものです。音声を聞いて空所を埋めましょう。

Some words in Japanese seem to be the same in meaning but (1.   ) in nuance. The Arabic numeral 0 is one example. This number can be (2.   ) in two ways; "zero" and "rei." Though their meaning is almost the same, their usage depends on circumstances.

First, when a Chinese character follows a number, the pronunciation of "rei" is used with expressions like "rei-ji" (zero hour, midnight) and "rei-do" (zero degrees), since "rei" is also the Chinese (3.   ).

Secondly, "rei" can mean a very small amount; this (4.   ) to the chance of rainfall in a weather forecast. If the (5.   ) of precipitation is four percent, then it is expressed as "rei" percent. This same usage of "rei" can be found in the expression "reisai-kigyo," meaning a very small company.

TIPS

「10進法」は「十進法」と書いた方が混乱しない？

「10」という表記は二進法では「2」を意味します。ですから「10進法」と表記すると、二進法が普通の世界では、「二進法」を意味することになります。

逆に、十二支などのように12個でひとまとまりになるカウントの方式を「12進法」という表記で表せば、これは通例、十進法の世界での表記です。12進法が普通の世界では、12番目に「10」という表記にならないといけないわけだから、この十二進法を表すには、やはり二進法の表記の場合と同様、「10進法」と表記しないといけなくなります。

というのは、十二進法とは、例えば、0, 1, 2, 3, 4, 5, 6, 7, 8. 9. P, Q, のように12種類の文字を用いて、12をカウントした途端に繰り上がって10となるからです。ちなみに、十二進法で12は、（十進法における）14を意味します。

上記で分かるように、何進法の世界でも、その方式をアラビア数字で表記すると「10進法」となるのです。そこで、「十進法」「十二進法」などと漢字で表した方が、混乱がないといえるでしょう。

UNIT 17　　How to Use Numbers in Japanese

 **Grammar Check**

次の英文の（　）内の語（句）のうち正しい方を選びましょう。

1. The number four is (pronouncing / pronounced) shi or yon in Japanese.
2. Most people say ichi, ni, san, shi when (to count / counting) up.
3. Adding a Chinese character (referred / referring) to time makes the phrase "reiji."
4. There is a phrase like "reisai kigyo," (meant / meaning) a very small company.
5. As (seen / to see) in the above explanation, understanding differences is important.
6. This is the (cause / reason) "rei" is used to express figures of precipitation probability.
7. The museum was full of people, as it usually (did / was) at this hour of the day.
8. I will gladly pay for the hotel if (you / you are) take care of the meal.
9. I did not do some research on it, because my teacher did not ask me (to / to do).
10. He buys a new tie only when his wife (makes him / makes him do).

一口文法　分詞

分詞は動詞の形を変化させたもので準動詞の1つである。-ing 形の現在分詞と -ed 形の過去分詞の2つがある。　　　　　　　　　　　　　　　　　[N= 名詞]

	句に関わる用法		文に関わる用法	
	形容詞的用法	副詞的用法	be +	have +
現在分詞	～している N	～しながら… ～したとき…など	[進行形] は～している	×
過去分詞	～された N	～されて… ～されたとき… など	[受動態] は～される	[完了形] 完了・経験 継続の意味

注1：分詞の副詞的用法を分詞構文と呼ぶ。
注2：ing 形に名詞的用法があるが、これは動名詞と呼び、分詞と区別する。
注3：分詞構文で意味上の主語が主文の主語と一致しない場合には、分詞の前に主語を示す。
　　　→ <u>There</u> being no bus service, we took a taxi.
　　　　（バスが運行していなかったので、タクシーを利用した）
注4：分詞構文の否定は、直前に not を入れ、完了形は having V-ed の形になる。

101

Writing Expressions

次の英文の（　　）内の単語を並べ替えて、英文を完成させましょう。

1. アラビア数字の0は日本語では、発音の方法が2つある。
   The Arabic numeral (in / is / pronounced / two / ways / 0) in Japanese.

   _____

2. ウサギが最初の糞（ふん）を食べるのは、何らかの意味があるものだ。
   (in / is / significance / some / that / there) rabbits eat some of their first dung.

   _____

3. この不思議なことの典型例の1つが，別の分野でも見つかる。
   One of (examples / mystery / of / the / this / typical) is found in another field.

   _____

4. 水が特別であることを示す例として，他に1つ挙げるなら、その固体が大きくなるということがある。
   Another (example / is / showing / special / that / water) is that its solid gets larger.

   _____

5. 上記の記述に見られるように、比較することによりすべてがはっきりする。
   (above / as / description / in / seen / the), comparison makes everything clear.

   _____

Discussion Topics

次の質問に答えることをきっかけとして、英語で話し合いましょう。

1. What is your favorite number? And why?

   _____

2. Find a word or phrase that is pronounced in two ways. How about one pronounced in three ways or more?

   _____

Japan Is Not a Small Country!

天武天皇の時代に「倭」(＝小さな国)から「日本」(＝日が昇る本[もと])というプラスイメージの国名になりました。しかし、今でも、日本は面積の視点から小さな国と見られています。でも、欧州諸国の中で日本より面積の大きな国は3カ国しかないという事実を知っていますか。この章では、小さな日本の大きな側面を学びましょう。

 Vocabulary Check

次の単語の定義を下の [a] ～ [h] から選びましょう。

(1) rank (　　)　　(2) incidentally (　　)　　(3) define (　　)
(4) surround (　　)　　(5) noteworthy (　　)　　(6) surpass (　　)
(7) decrease (　　)　　(8) contribution (　　)

[a] to be greater or to do better than something or somebody
[b] to make something become smaller in size, number, amount, quality, etc.
[c] deserving to be noticed due to importance, interest or uniqueness
[d] by the way
[e] an action, service or situation that helps to cause or develop something
[f] to be around something or somebody
[g] to say the meaning of a word or phrase; to describe something precisely
[h] to give a particular position on a scale based on quantity, quality or importance

Generally speaking, Japan is a small country in terms of area. Japan has a total surface area of 377,972 km², which ranks 62nd in the world. The total land area of the world is 148,940,000 km², so Japan occupies only 0.25% of the world. Incidentally, the total land area of the world corresponds to about 29.1% of the surface area of the Earth.

There are 197 countries in the world now, so though Japan is very small, 135 countries are even smaller than Japan. The smallest country in the world is Vatican City, having an area of only 0.44 km², while the world's smallest island country is Nauru, with an area of 21 km².

Japan is also an island country made up of 6,852 islands, including the four main islands. The prefecture with the largest number of islands is Nagasaki, with 971. In this case, "island" is defined as a landmass surrounded by water and with a coastline of more than 100 meters. The country with the largest number of islands is Indonesia, with about 17,500, followed by the Philippines with about 7,100. Japan ranks third in this category.

Especially noteworthy is the fact that in Europe, there are only three countries larger than Japan, which are Spain, France, and Sweden.

As for population, Japan is at 11th place, with a total population of 126,570,000 as of 2016. At present, the total population of the world is approximately 7.3 billion.

China has the largest population of the world with 1,383,920,000 people, while India ranks second with 1,311,050,000 people. Astonishingly, these two countries occupy 37% of the total population of the world, which means at least one out of three people in the world is Chinese or Indian.

In 2016, Mexico surpassed Japan in population. Now Mexico ranks 10th with a population of 127,010,000, with the Philippines coming in behind Japan with 107,000,000 people. There are only 12 countries in the world whose

UNIT 18 *Japan Is Not a Small Country!*

population is greater than 100,000,000.

Japan's population is decreasing annually; however, the population of the world as a whole is increasing at a rate of about 140 people per minute. Therefore, it is estimated that in 2100, the total world population will surpass 10 billion people.

5

We can say that Japanese are fish-loving people considering the amount of fish they consume. According to some data, Japanese eat 30% of the world's total catch of fish. To be more specific, they eat 70% of the total catch of eels, two thirds of the world's octopi, and a third of the squid caught on Earth. Japan, though small in area, exercises great influence on the world from contributions 10 to technology to keeping fishermen the world over happy.

Notes

Vatican City バチカン市国 / **total catch of fish** 全漁獲量 / **octopi** [複数] タコ ⇒単数形は octopus

* · · · * · · · * · · * · · * · · · * · · · * · · * · · · * · · · * · · · * · · · * · · *

T/F Questions

次の英文が本文の内容と一致する場合は T、一致しない場合は F を記入しましょう。

1. [   ] The area of Japan is only one 400th of the total area of the world.

2. [   ] The world's smallest country has an area of 21 km².

3. [   ] Nagasaki Prefecture, with 971 islands, ranks second in the list of Japanese prefectures with a large number of islands.

4. [   ] China and India occupy 37% of the total population of the world.

5. [   ] One third of the world's total catch of squid is eaten by Japanese.

105

次の英文パッセージは本文を要約したものです。音声を聞いて空所を埋めましょう。

　　Among the 197 countries of the world, Japan is a (1.　　　　　) very small country but only three nations in Europe are larger than Japan: Spain, France, and Sweden. All other European countries are smaller than Japan. Japan (2.　　　　　　　　) 62nd in the world in terms of area.

　　However, regarding population, Japan comes into (3.　　　　　) place between Mexico and the Philippines.

　　Japan can be proud of its (4.　　　　　　) islands, the third most in the world. Indonesia has the largest number with about 17,500, followed by the Philippines with about 7,100.

　　Japan may be small but its people make their (5.　　　　　　) known. For example, Japanese eat 30% of the world's total catch of fish. Astonishingly, they eat 70% of the total catch of eels.

TIPS

日本は義務教育の学校のほとんどにプールがある珍しい国

　日本の小学校で87.8%、中学校で72.2%の学校がプールを持っています(2008年度)が、実は、多くの学校にプールがあるという国はほとんどありません。四方を海で囲まれた日本は、江戸時代から水泳の訓練（水練）がありました。

　17世紀ごろ、日新館（会津藩[現在の福島県]の藩校）と明倫館（長州藩[現在の山口県]の藩校）が最初の水練場を作ったといわれています。1952年に水難事故が相次ぎ、さらに、1955年には修学旅行生を乗せた紫雲丸が大型貨物船と衝突して100人以上の生徒が亡くなる事故があったことで、水泳の授業が必修となりました。

UNIT 18   *Japan Is Not a Small Country!*

Grammar Check

次の英文の (   ) に入る適切な単語を、下の枠内から選びましょう。選択肢のなかには、使用しないものも含まれています。

1. Japan (   ) only 0.25% of the world in terms of area.

2. The world as a whole is (   ) its population at the rate of 140 people a minute.

3. It is (   ) that in 2100, the total world population will surpass 10 billion people.

4. He is not careful in nature but now he is (   ) careful, since his teacher advised him.

5. She usually did not wear a red ribbon, but she was (   ) it at the recent party.

6. Especially (   ) is the fact that only three European countries are larger than Japan.

7. On the cliff (   ) a temple in which a secret Buddha is housed.

8. Under no circumstances will she try to (   ) something challenging; she is brave.

9. Living as she (   ) near the art museum, she could see plenty of wonderful pictures.

10. (   ) he helped me a lot when I was in trouble, I would be more successful now.

| avoid   being   did   estimated   had   increased   increasing |
| noteworthy   occupying   occupies   stands   conquer   wearing |

一口文法   **倒置構文**

通常の平叙文の語順と異なる語順になる特殊な構文で、以下のような種類がある。

種類	例文
CVS	Even more important is this. （もっと重要なのはこれだ）
MVS	On the hill stands a castle. （丘の上に建っているのは城だ）
否定副詞 (句)+v S V	Never have I met her. （彼女に会ったことは決してない）
程度副詞 (句)+v S V	Well do I remember the scene. （その光景はよく覚えている）
V-ing ～ is X	Standing there is a girl. （そこに立っているのは１人の少女だ）
OSV	Mary, John loves. （メアリーはジョンが愛している）
if 省略節	Were I you, I would do so. （私があなたならそうするよ）
副詞節 (as 節)	Try as you may, it'll be hard. （いくらやっても難しいよ）
譲歩副詞節 (what 節)	Come what may, I will do so. （何が起ころうとそうします）

注：as 節は譲歩節のみ倒置が可能とは限らない。doing as ～ do で「実際～は do しているので」や done as ～ is で「実際～が do されているので」という理由節も倒置可能。

107

Writing Expressions

次の英文の（　　）内の単語を並べ替えて、英文を完成させましょう。

1. 北海道の面積は，日本全体の面積の約22％に相当する。
   The area of Hokkaido (about / corresponds / of / the / to / 22%) total area of Japan.

   _____

2. 最近の研究によると、人間の体は37兆個の細胞から成っている。
   The recent study shows that the human body (is / made / of / trillion / up / 37) cells.

   _____

3. 特に注目すべきことは、人体には270種類の細胞があるという事実である。
   (especially / fact / is / noteworthy / that / the) our body has 270 kinds of cells.

   _____

4. 日本人の2人に1人ががんを発症し、3人に1人ががんで死亡する。
   One out of two Japanese suffers from cancer (and / dies / of / one / out / three) of it.

   _____

5. ＡＩ技術の発達は、人間の未来の生活に確実に多大な影響を与えるだろう。
   The development of AI technology will surely (exercise / future / great / humans' / influence / on) life.

   _____

Discussion Topics

次の質問に答えることをきっかけとして、英語で話し合いましょう。

1. What Japanese thing do you think you can be most proud of? And why?

   _____

2. Where would you take a foreign visitor if you are asked to take him or her to a very beautiful or impressive place in Japan?

   _____

The Sea of Japan

『日本書紀』の垂仁天皇２年の記述に「北海を回って出雲国を経て」というのがあるので、古代には日本海を北海と呼んでいたのが分かります。日本は4,000万年前まではユーラシア大陸と陸続きでしたが、2,000万年前までに大陸から徐々に分離するにつれ、古代の北海、すなわち、日本海が形成されました。意外とよく知らない日本海について学びましょう。

Vocabulary Check

次の単語の定義を下の [a] 〜 [h] から選びましょう。

(1) border (　　)　　(2) square (　　)　　(3) interrupt (　　)
(4) outstanding (　　)　(5) monsoon (　　)　(6) southerly (　　)
(7) blow (　　)　　　(8) deposit (　　)

[a] so good as to stand out from others of its kind
[b] from the south, used especially of wind
[c] a line where one country or area ends and another begins
[d] to send out a strong current of air
[e] a large amount of mineral in the rock or in the ground
[f] to make it impossible for something to go smoothly
[g] a figure having four angles and four sides that are all the same length
[h] a seasonal wind in southern Asia blowing from the southwest in summer and from the northeast in winter; rainy season in southern Asia in general

The Sea of Japan, or Nihon-kai, also called the East Sea, is bordered by Japan and Sakhalin Island to the east and by mainland Asia to the west. Its area is 377,600 square miles (978,000 km^2). It has an average depth of 5,748 feet (1,752 m) and a maximum depth of 12,276 feet (3,742 m).

The sea is almost elliptical and has its major axis spanning from southwest to northeast. Its northern boundary lies at latitude 51°45' N, while to the south it is demarcated by a line drawn from the Japanese island of Kyushu westward through the Gotō Islands of Japan to the Korean Peninsula.

The sea itself lies in a deep basin and is separated from the East China Sea to the south by the Tsushima and Korea straits. To the east it is also connected with the Inland Sea of Japan by the Kanmon Strait, and to the Pacific by the Tsugaru Strait.

The four straits connecting the sea either to the Pacific Ocean or to marginal seas were formed in recent geologic periods. The oldest of these are the Tsugaru and Tsushima straits, whose formation interrupted the migration of elephants to the Japanese islands at the end of the Neogene period (about 2.6 million years ago).

The Sea of Japan influences the climate of Japan because of its relatively warm waters; evaporation is especially outstanding in winter, when a massive quantity of water vapor rises in the region between the cold, dry polar air mass and the warm, moist tropical air mass. In mid-winter, the prevailing northwest monsoon wind carries cold and dry continental polar air masses over the warmer waters of the sea. As a result, it snows quite heavily along the mountainous western coasts of Japan. In summer the southerly tropical monsoon blows from the Pacific onto the Asian mainland, causing heavy fog when its warm and moist winds pass over the cold currents.

In terms of its economic impact, fish and mineral deposits are the most

UNIT 19   *The Sea of Japan*

popular resources derived from the Sea of Japan. Oceanic fish include types of mackerel, sardines, anchovies, herring, fish of the salmon and trout family, sea bream, and squid; while deep sea and bottom dwellers include cod, Japanese bluefish, and Atka mackerel. Seals and whales are also to be found, as well as crustaceans such as shrimp and crabs.　　　　　　　　　　　　　　　　　　　5

　　　The waters of the Sea of Japan have been traveled for centuries. Historically, they have served to protect Japan from foreign invasions. European exploration in the region began in the 18th century. In the 1780s, in one of the first voyages, some European countries made efforts to search for new trade opportunities along the Sea of Japan and collected scientific data.　　　　10

Notes

Sakhalin サハリン / **elliptical** 楕円形の / **latitude** 緯度 / **demarcate** 区別する；〜の境界を定める / **basin** 海盆（かいぼん：円形またはだ円状の海底のくぼ地）/ **marginal sea** 縁海（えんかい：大陸の外縁にあって、列島や半島で不完全に大洋から区画されている海）/ **geologic** 地質学上の / **migration** 移住 / **Neogene period** 新第三紀 / **air mass** 気団 / **tropical monsoon** 熱帯季節風 / **cold current** 寒流 / **mackerel** サバ / **anchovies** カタクチイワシ / **herring** ニシン / **sea bream** タイ　/ **Japanese bluefish** ムツ / **Atka mackerel** ホッケ / **crustacean** 甲殻類

◖◗ T/F Questions

次の英文が本文の内容と一致する場合は T、一致しない場合は F を記入しましょう。

1. [　　] The Sea of Japan is not separated from the East China Sea by any straits.

2. [　　] The oldest of the four straits mentioned here are the Kanmon Strait and Tsugaru Strait.

3. [　　] The Sea of Japan affects the climate of Japan due to its relatively warm waters.

4. [　　] Water evaporates in large amounts in winter.

5. [　　] It snows a lot along the western seacoasts of Japan.

111

次の英文パッセージは本文を要約したものです。音声を聞いて空所を埋めましょう。

The Sea of Japan is (1. _____) by Japan and Sakhalin Island to the east and by the Asian nations to the west. To the east it is also (2. _____) with the Inland Sea of Japan by the Kanmon Strait, and to the Pacific by the Tsugaru Strait.

The Sea of Japan (3. _____) the climate of Japan because of its relatively warm waters; evaporation is especially prevalent in winter.

As for its economic (4. _____), fish and mineral deposits are the main (5. _____) in this sea. The waters of the Sea of Japan have been traveled for centuries, and historically they have served to protect Japan from foreign invasions.

TIPS

日本の海の驚きの数字

日本の200カイリ以内（日本近海）において、これまでに確認された生物の種類は33,629種もあります。これは、世界25海域で1位です。世界に生息する全海洋生物は約25万種存在するので、その約13.5％が日本近海に分布していることになります。

日本近海の容積は、全海洋の0.9％に満たないにもかかわらず、これだけ多くの種類の生物が生息しているわけですから、日本近海は正に生物の宝庫と言えます。

この理由は、生息環境の多様性にあると考えられます。例えば、日本は南北に長く、北には流氷、南にはサンゴ礁があり、9,000ｍを超える超深海があり、海流は暖流と寒流が合流し、海底では4枚のプレートがぶつかり合っていることが、種の多様性を生み出しているのです。

UNIT 19   *The Sea of Japan*

Grammar Check

次の英文の (   ) 内に当てはまる正しい単語を書き入れましょう。

1. The Sea of Japan is bordered (　　　　) Japan and Sakhalin Island to the east.

2. It is separated (　　　　) the East China Sea by the Tsushima and Korea straits.

3. Seals and whales are also to (　　　　) found, as well as shrimp and crabs.

4. Many marine animals are taken good care (　　　　) by caretakers at the aquarium

5. The matter (　　　) been deeply looked into by researchers until quite recently.

6. The waters of the Sea of Japan have been traveled (　　　　) centuries.

7. The raging waves of the sea have served to protect Japan (　　　　) foreign invasions.

8. "Have you (　　　　) been to the country?" "No, I have never been there, I'm afraid."

9. When we arrived at the bus stop, the bus (　　　　) already left, so we had to take a taxi.

10. I (　　　　) have read the book by next Monday, so I can lend it to you next Tuesday.

一口文法　**完了形**

完了形は＜ have ＋過去分詞＞で表される。一般に完了・経験・継続の意味を持つ。
時制の観点からは、現在完了・過去完了・未来完了がある。それぞれ、現在・過去・未来を基準にして、それ以前の時制と関わっていることを示す。

	現在完了	過去完了	未来完了	よく使われる語句
完了	〜してしまった	〜してしまっていた	〜してしまうことになる	already, just not … yet
経験	〜したことがある	〜したことがあった	〜したことになる	… times ever, before
継続	ずっと〜している	ずっと〜していた	〜していることになる	for … hours/years since …

注 1：明確な過去を表す表現は、現在完了とともに用いることはできない。

→ × Mary has left <u>a few minutes ago</u>.

注 2：次の違いに注意する。

(1)　a. ○ I haven't seen her this morning. [昼ごろまでの発言]

　　　b. ○ I didn't see her this morning. [昼すぎの発言]

(2)　a. Her grandfather has lived here all his life. [祖父はまだ健在]

　　　b. Her grandfather lived here all his life. [祖父はすでに死亡]

113

Writing Expressions

次の英文の（　　）内の単語を並べ替えて、英文を完成させましょう。

1. 日本海を、太平洋または複数の縁海に接続している海峡が４つある。
   There are four straits connecting the Sea of Japan (either / Ocean / or / Pacific / the / to) to marginal seas.

2. 実験が明確に示したことは、被験者に書かれたものを音読させることが、後の記憶力にプラスに影響するということである。
   Experiments have demonstrated that making a subject read (aloud / influences / is / positively / what / written) his or her later memory.

3. 南極の氷が解けても、それに応じて、周りの海の大量の水が蒸発するため、水位は上がらないという説がある。
   There is a theory that even if Antarctic ice melts, the water level will not rise due (a / massive / of / quantity / to / water) in the surrounding seas evaporating accordingly.

4. 「こころ」という言葉は、「凝る」という動詞の古い形である「ここる」から派生したようだ。
   The word "kokoro" (been / derived / from / have / seems / to) "kokoru," or the older form of the verb "koru" meaning "stiffen."

5. ホモサピエンスは氷河期に南下し、好奇心から貝などの新たな食べ物を探したが、このことによってうまく生き延びることができた。
   During the glacial period, Homo sapiens went (for / new / search / some / southward / to) food like shellfish out of curiosity, which successfully led to their survival.

Discussion Topics

次の質問に答えることをきっかけとして、英語で話し合いましょう。

1. Which do you like better, the sea or mountains? And why?

2. Have you ever been to a region along the Sea of Japan? If so, tell me about the region.

The Mystery of 36

色では青、数字では７が好まれる傾向があるようです。確かに「ラッキーセブン」と言ったりします。でも、日本では、漢字で書けば末広がりとなる「八」が好まれたりします。数字は影響力を持っていると言えるでしょう。何でもない数字に着目すると、意外とすごいことが分かってきます。今回は３６という数字に着目します。この数字のすごさを味わいましょう。

Vocabulary Check

次の単語の定義を下の [a] 〜 [h] から選びましょう。

(1) confuse (　　)　　(2) peak (　　)　　(3) abundance (　　)
(4) sequence (　　)　　(5) equation (　　)　　(6) angle (　　)
(7) respiration (　　)　　(8) combine (　　)

[a] the act of breathing
[b] a large amount that is more than enough
[c] to think wrongly that something is something else
[d] the pointed top of a mountain; a mountain with a pointed top
[e] the space between two lines which is measured in degrees
[f] to join two or more things together to form one particular thing
[g] a statement that two different values are the same
[h] a set of actions, events, or numbers that have a particular order

The Japanese artist, Katsushika Hokusai, completed a series of popular woodblock prints known as the "Thirty-six Views of Mt. Fuji." This should not be confused with the "Thirty-six Peaks of Eastern Mountains," which refers to 36 peaks located in Kyoto: the first peak being that of Mt. Hiei, whose monasteries were established for the Tendai sect of Buddhism started by Saicho; the last peak being that of Mt. Inari, famous for its Fushimi Inari Shrine.

It may seem unusual that such a specific number as 36 was chosen in both instances. The number is relatively large, compared with three or ten, which are more often used to represent groupings. The reason is simple, though; this number is quite special.

First, this number is characterized by its abundance of divisors, which are one, two, three, four, six, nine, twelve, eighteen, and thirty-six. Therefore, thirty-six can be divided by those numbers, resulting in an integer.

Moreover, if you add whole numbers from one to eight, then you get 36. If you add a sequence of the first six odd numbers from one through eleven, you get 36 again. Also, the sum of the first prime quadruplets is 36. Furthermore, the product of the first two prime numbers squared results in 36. The equations are as follows:

$$1 + 2 + 3 + 4 + 5 + 6 + 7 + 8 = 36$$
$$1 + 3 + 5 + 7 + 9 + 11 = 36$$
$$5 + 7 + 11 + 13 = 36$$
$$(2 \times 2) \times (3 \times 3) = 2^2 \times 3^2 = 36$$

If you use the first three numbers (1, 2, 3), the following equations are also possible.

$$1^2 \times 2^2 \times 3^2 = 1^3 + 2^3 + 3^3 = 36$$
$$(1 + 2 + 3)^2 = (1 \times 2 \times 3)^2 = 36$$

Thirty-six is also significant in geometry. Rotating a line from a single point makes a circle at 360 degrees. Each of the angles of the five corners of a pentagram is 36 degrees. The low angle of an isosceles triangle in which the ratio of its side to its base is the golden ratio is also 36 degrees.

The total number of Arabic numerals and the letters of the English alphabet is 36, which only allows a numbering system based on 36 theoretically. 5

Mathematically, thirty-six is an interesting number, but this number also seems important medically. For example, the human body's temperature is usually around 36 degrees Celsius, when healthy. The average respiration rate for a minute happens to be 18, half of 36. Moreover, the average pulse rate per minute of men and women combined is approximately 72, or double the 10 number 36.

The number 36 is really a mysterious number. It could even be said that the first 36 seconds is important while giving lectures. Within this length of time, the speaker should make the audience laugh or impress them deeply, to help maintain their interest in the talk. 15

If you count the number of times that 36 was mentioned in this piece … no, just kidding! It's not 36!

Notes

woodblock print 木版画（浮世絵のこと）/ **Thirty-six Peaks of Eastern Mountains** 東山三十六峰（京都盆地の東部を区切る南北 12 キロに及ぶ 36 の山々：比叡山から稲荷山まで）/ **divisor** 約数 / **integer** 整数 / **odd number** 奇数 / **prime quadruplet** 四つ子素数（[p, p+2, p+6, p+8] の形式の素数の組、p ＝ 5 が最初の四つ子素数）/ **pentagram** 五角星形（星型正五角形）/ **low angle** 底角 / **isosceles triangle** 二等辺三角形 / **golden ratio** 黄金比 / **Celsius** セ氏 / **a numbering system based on 36** 36 進法 / **pulse** 脈拍

T/F Questions

次の英文が本文の内容と一致する場合は T、一致しない場合は F を記入しましょう。

1. [   ] The 36th peak of "Thirty-six Peaks of Eastern Mountains" is Mt. Hiei.
2. [   ] The number of divisors of 36 is nine.
3. [   ] The addition of a sequence of the first six prime numbers is 36.
4. [   ] Thirty-six seems to be an important number in the medical field, too.
5. [   ] The author says that the first 36 minutes is important in lectures.

Summary Listening

次の英文パッセージは本文を要約したものです。音声を聞いて空所を埋めましょう。

Thirty-six is a very special number for several reasons. First, it has an (1.   ) of divisors. It can be divided by one, two, three, four, six, nine, twelve, eighteen and thirty-six.

Second, the sum of whole numbers from one to eight is 36. The total of the first six (2.   ) numbers is also 36. The sum of the first prime quadruplets is 36 again. In this way, we can think of a variety of (3.   ) from a mathematical point of view.

Coincidentally, this number (4.   ) some significance in a biological sense. The human body's temperature is approximately 36 degrees Celsius. The average respiration rate for a minute is half the number 36, 18. The average (5.   ) rate per minute is double the number, at 72.

TIPS

うろこが 36 個あるコイが成長すると、うろこが 81 個の竜になる！

　コイはかつて六六鱗（ろくろくりん）と呼ばれ、約 36 個のうろこが側線 (lateral line) 上にあります。コイは滝を登って竜に成長するという中国の故事がありますが、竜は九九鱗（くくりん）と呼ばれ、81 個のうろこがあるとされています。

　81 のうろこのうち、あごの下にある一枚の逆さに生えているうろこを逆鱗（げきりん）と言い、これに触れると、竜は怒ったという故事に基づき、目上の人を怒らせたときに、「逆鱗に触れる」という表現が使われるようになりました。

UNIT 20   *The Mystery of 36*

⬤ Grammar Check

次の英文の（　）内に当てはまる単語を書き入れましょう。［1 ～ 4 は関係詞］

1. We mention "Higashiyama 36 Peaks," (　　　　　) refers to 36 peaks located in Kyoto.

2. The first peak is that of Mt. Hiei, (　　　　　) monasteries were built for the Tendai sect.

3. There's an isosceles triangle in (　　　　　) the ratio of its side to its base is the golden ratio.

4. Tell me about the book (　　　　) you have which is of great help for my research.

5. I'll tell you about the dictionary that I think (　　　　　) very useful for your study.

6. The boss made me work overtime, so I had to do so though I did not want (　　　　).

7. She was made (　　　　) study hard by her teacher, since she was absent for a month.

8. I (　　　　　) my homework done by my brother yesterday; he is always of great help to me.

9. My father (　　　　) me study abroad, since I asked him earnestly to allow me to do so.

10. This medicine will (　　　　　) you feel better if you take it three times a day after a meal.

> **一口文法**　　**関係詞その 2 「whose+ 名詞」と「which ＋名詞」の違い**
>
> (a)　They climbed a mountain whose name I didn't know.
>   [whose は関係代名詞所有格]
>   彼らは、私が知らない名前の山に登った。
>   [=They climbed a mountain and I didn't know its name.
>   [and ＋ its → whose]
> (b)　They climbed Mt. Baka, which name I didn't know.
>   [which は関係形容詞]
>   彼らはバカ山に登った。そしてそんな名前を私は知らなかった。
>   [=They climbed Mt. Baka, and I didn't know that name.
>   [and ＋ that → which]

Writing Expressions

次の英文の（　　）内の単語を並べ替えて、英文を完成させましょう。

1. 阿蘇山は5つの山（五岳）から成っていて、最も高い山は高岳で標高1,592mである。
   Mt. Aso consists of 5 peaks, (being / highest / peak / the / the / 1592m-high) Takadake.

   _____

2. コイの特徴はその長寿で、150年以上生きるコイもいるだろう。
   (are / by / carp / characterized / longevity / their); some may live for over 150 years.

   _____

3. 和が6で積が−16の2つの整数は何か。
   Find the two integers, the sum of which is 6 (and / is / of / product / the / which) -16.

   _____

4. 円周率とは円周の直径に対する比である。
   Pi is the ratio of (a / circle / circumference / of / the / to) its diameter.

   _____

5. メンデルの法則に基づく遺伝の理論について教えてください。
   Teach me about (based / inheritance / of / on / the / theory) Mendel's laws.

   _____

Discussion Topics

次の質問に答えることをきっかけとして、英語で話し合いましょう。

1. What number do you think has the greatest influence on Japanese culture? And why?

   _____

2. What would you choose if you are asked what the three most important things for college students are?

   _____